Dear Joy

I benefitted immensely from the Sonia Choquette book about trusting our Sixth Sense. I hope you get as much from this book.

Happy 49th Birthday

Love Mum

12th April 2006

P.S. Love the exercises P80 onwards. They seem to work on humans too.

Beyond Barks
The Art of Canine Telepathy for Dog Trainers

Prologue

"A dog is the only thing on earth that loves you more than he loves himself."

— Josh Billings

Dedication

For my sweet dog-loving sister, Ulla Saxine

Table of Contents

Introduction: Unlocking the Mysteries of Canine Communication 7

Chapter 1: Understanding the Unspoken Bond 11

Chapter 2: The Science and Spirit of Communication 16

Chapter 3: Canine Intuition: Fact, Folklore, and Phenomea 21

Chapter Four: The Role of Evolution in Canine Communication 28

Chapter Five: Non-Verbal Cues in Training and Daily Life 34

Chapter Seven: Visualization and "Sending": Communication Without Words 47

Chapter Eight: Dogs in Human Lives: Guardians, Healers, and Partners 54

Chapter Ten: Exploring Skepticism -A Balanced Perspective 66

Chapter Eleven: A Holistic Approach to Living with Dogs 70

Chapter Twelve: Closing Thoughts – Embracing The Mystery of Connection 74

Sources: 77

Appendix with Exercises and More 79

Leash up and lead!

Introduction: Unlocking the Mysteries of Canine Communication

There's a universal thrill in the bond between humans and dogs—a connection that feels almost as old as time itself. If you've ever shared a look with your dog and felt as though you both understood something beyond words, you've likely tapped into a mystery that countless dog owners experience but can hardly explain. Could it be that dogs are picking up on our thoughts? Are they sensing things in ways we don't fully understand? And could these moments of shared awareness be something we can cultivate and even refine?

This book is an invitation to explore these questions through stories, science, and practical tools. We'll journey into the heart of what makes the connection between humans and dogs so special, weaving together insights from psychology, animal behavior, and even the age-old lore surrounding animals' "sixth sense." This bond isn't just about commands and obedience—it's about understanding, empathy, and an unspoken language that some may even call telepathy.

I remember the first time I experienced this connection as a child. At the age of seven, I found myself entering a world usually reserved for adults—the world of competitive dog handling. I was blond, skinny, not too tall, and certainly not the most experienced in a ring full of towering adults and their large, highly-trained dogs. Yet there I stood, beside my young, red, long-haired dachshund, Baline. To everyone's surprise, including my own, we won. It felt like an underdog story, a victory shaped by more than just skill—there was an unspoken bond between us, an attunement I couldn't explain but deeply felt. Looking back, I realize that moment was the beginning of a lifelong fascination with canine communication.

The journey to understand this bond has led to fascinating discoveries. Throughout history, we've heard of dogs sensing danger, alerting their owners to fires, detecting illnesses, and even comforting people through grief. Stories abound of dogs warning their owners of an approaching earthquake, or, like in Thailand in 2004, sounding the alarm just before the catastrophic tsunami hit, guiding people to safety. And it's not only dogs; herds of animals have been known to coordinate effortlessly, as if moving to the beat of a silent, shared signal, highlighting a kind of group intelligence that defies easy explanation.

Then there are the more personal stories—moments when our dogs appear to pick up on our emotions or needs as though they have access to our innermost thoughts. One story from my family speaks to this mystery. We had a dog who had run away and was lost for quite some time. Then, one day, my grandmother shared a dream in which she saw him in a forest, something about a star guiding her vision. That very day, we received a call from a forest ranger who'd found the dog—at a place called *The North Star*, deep in a forest miles away. How did she know? Was it coincidence, intuition, or something more?

In exploring this shared awareness, we'll discuss insights from both science and history. Concepts like remote viewing, once part of secret government programs, reveal how deeply the human mind is connected to intuition. Though it may sound unusual, the U.S. military invested in researching this phenomenon, developing ways for people to expand their natural intuition, refining what some might call a sixth sense. The human brain, after all, takes in millions of bits of information every second—far more than we're consciously aware of. Some researchers suggest that our brains, like those of dogs, may already be "wired" to receive and interpret signals that lie beneath the surface of our awareness.

Antoine de Saint-Exupéry once wrote, "It is only with the heart that one can see rightly; what is essential is invisible to the eye." This book is grounded in that spirit. We don't need to prove or disprove the mystery of canine telepathy to appreciate its beauty. Instead, we can allow ourselves to be curious and open, exploring the world of intuition alongside our dogs, learning to see them not just as pets, but as partners in an ancient, shared adventure.

As you read, I hope this book offers both practical insights and a sense of wonder. Whether you're looking to strengthen your bond with your dog, enhance your understanding of their behaviors, or simply enjoy the stories of animals who "just know," you'll find something valuable here. Together, we'll explore how to embrace the mystery and beauty of this connection, and perhaps even learn something new about our own intuitive capacities in the process.

Let's embark on this journey with open minds and hearts, ready to listen, observe, and connect with our dogs in ways we may have only dreamed of before.

Chapter 1: Understanding the Unspoken Bond

"Dogs are not our whole life, but they make our lives whole." —Roger Caras

Every dog owner knows the feeling: a silent glance from your dog, a wag of the tail, or a subtle shift in posture—and suddenly, you understand each other. It's almost magical how a creature of another species can communicate without words, yet feel so familiar, so close. This connection goes beyond mere affection or companionship; it taps into something deeper, almost as if we're speaking a language we don't entirely understand.

The relationship between humans and dogs is unique in the animal kingdom.

Psychologist and animal behaviorist Dr. Stanley Coren, who has written extensively on dog intelligence, describes dogs as "non-verbal geniuses." According to Coren (1994), dogs can understand hundreds of words, gestures, and tones, often responding to subtle cues we don't even realize we're giving. He suggests that dogs are finely attuned to our body language, a skill honed over thousands of years of domestication and close partnership with humans.

Yet, anyone who has shared a life with a dog might feel there's more to this connection than body language and learned responses. Perhaps you've experienced moments where your dog seems to know what you're thinking or feeling. This phenomenon is sometimes brushed off as anthropomorphism, the human tendency to project our thoughts and emotions onto animals. But countless stories suggest there may be more to it.

Take, for example, the story of Hachiko, the famously loyal Akita in Japan. Hachiko continued to wait at the Shibuya train station for his owner, a professor, every day for nearly ten years after the man's death. While loyalty is often touted as a primary trait of dogs, the question remains: how did Hachiko know to keep coming back to that same spot, day after day? Was it routine? Or was there a deeper, unexplainable drive at work? Such stories resonate with us because they hint at something more profound, a type of understanding or communication that transcends explanation.

The Science of Canine Perception

Scientists have studied dogs' abilities to pick up on human cues, and the results are fascinating. Dr. Brian Hare, an evolutionary anthropologist at Duke University, has explored the concept of "dognition" in his research. Hare's work suggests that dogs have evolved special cognitive skills that allow them to understand human gestures and intentions better than even our closest relatives, the chimpanzees (Hare & Tomasello, 2005). It's almost as if dogs are biologically wired to comprehend us.

But this wiring goes beyond understanding simple gestures or commands. Hare's research indicates that dogs can pick up on complex emotional states. In one study, dogs responded differently to humans based on whether the person was smiling or frowning (Tate, 2008). Dogs have even been shown to "catch" emotions from humans, mirroring our moods in a way reminiscent of empathy. They seem to have a unique ability to read the invisible currents of our emotional lives, which strengthens the bond we feel with them.

Yet science often hesitates to tread into the realm of "sixth sense." Tales of dogs sensing impending earthquakes, fires, or other disasters have been widely documented. In Thailand, just hours before the 2004 tsunami struck, elephants, dogs, and other animals fled to higher ground, alerting some villagers who followed them to safety. It's believed that these animals were able to detect subsonic waves generated by the approaching tsunami—an ability beyond human perception. Dogs, too, have demonstrated this kind of perception, leading some researchers to investigate the biological basis of these "intuitive" behaviors (Seymour et al., 2019).

Could it be, then, that dogs' ability to sense our emotions and needs taps into a similar channel? While they may not predict natural disasters every day, their sensitivity to us is undeniable, and perhaps, like the animals in Thailand, they're attuned to subtleties in their environment that are usually invisible to us.

The Role of Shared Intuition

There's an old idea in psychology known as "attunement," which describes how people in close relationships can become sensitive to each other's emotions and thoughts. This concept, explored in depth by psychologist Daniel Stern (1985), suggests that people can "tune in" to each other's inner states, building a bond that feels almost telepathic. Attunement has long been studied in human relationships, especially between parents and infants, but it can easily extend to our relationships with animals.

Our dogs often seem to attune to our emotions without needing words, a phenomenon many dog owners report experiencing daily. The poet Antoine de Saint-Exupéry wrote, "It is only with the heart that one can see rightly; what is essential is invisible to the eye." This sense of "seeing" with the heart might explain why some of us feel that our dogs understand us in ways other humans don't. It's not that they can read our minds, necessarily, but they sense our emotions, our energy, our subtle cues, and respond to them in ways that can feel astonishingly perceptive.

My own family has experienced this kind of attunement in uncanny ways. We had a dog who would sit upright at the sound of footsteps no one else could hear. Sometimes, in the middle of the night, I would wake to the distinct patter of small feet on our polished wooden floors. No one else heard it, yet our dog would sit up, his ears perked in alertness, following an invisible presence that I too sensed but couldn't see. Whether it was a shared experience or something only he could perceive, it left me wondering about the extent of his sensitivity, a sensitivity that connected us in those quiet, almost mystical hours.

Dogs and the Power of Presence

One possible explanation for this sensitivity lies in the concept of mindfulness. Dogs live in the present moment, attuned to what's happening around them with a degree of focus that humans often struggle to maintain. Psychologists have noted that mindfulness—being present and fully engaged with the here and now—can increase our sensitivity to others and even our surroundings. Dogs, by nature, exist in this state, which may contribute to their heightened awareness and intuition.

Interestingly, some researchers believe that humans can strengthen their own intuition by adopting this "present-moment" approach, often through practices like meditation and mindfulness (Siegel, 2007). Training ourselves to stay present could allow us to "meet" our dogs on their level, becoming more aware of the subtle ways they communicate with us. By learning to be still and listen, we may find that our own senses sharpen, and the bond we share with our dogs grows deeper.

Seeing with the Heart

As we delve deeper into the ways dogs communicate, it becomes clear that our connection with them is complex and multi-dimensional. They communicate not only through their bodies, but through an attuned awareness of our energy, moods, and presence. If we approach this bond with an open heart and a willingness to learn, we may find ourselves in the company of a partner who understands us better than we realize.

Exploring this unspoken bond isn't about proving a scientific theory; it's about embracing the mystery that allows us to feel closer to our dogs and, in doing so, to a part of ourselves. By tapping into their world, even just a little, we may uncover new ways to strengthen our connection, communicate with empathy, and appreciate the profound companionship they offer.

Our journey into this world of shared intuition has only just begun. As we explore further, we'll begin to understand how our own awareness, intuition, and even mindfulness can open doors to a richer relationship with our dogs—one that goes beyond words and touches something much deeper.

Chapter 2: The Science and Spirit of Communication

How Dogs Understand Us: Vocal, Body Language, and Scent Cues

Communication with our dogs can feel incredibly intuitive, yet it's built on specific channels— our voices, gestures, and even scents. Dogs possess an extraordinary ability to read and respond to these cues, but their comprehension goes beyond mere commands. They seem to grasp intention, recognize our emotional states, and react in ways that strengthen our bond with them.

In recent studies, dogs were shown to respond not only to the tone of human voices but also to individual words (Andics et al., 2016). Researchers at Eötvös Loránd University in Budapest used MRI scanning to observe brain activity in dogs when listening to speech. They found that dogs process words and intonation in separate brain hemispheres, similar to humans. This ability to distinguish meaning from both words and tone reflects a sophisticated level of communication.

However, vocal cues are just one piece of the puzzle. Dogs are astute observers of body language, reacting to subtle changes in posture and movement. If a dog owner leans forward slightly, their dog might interpret this as an invitation to engage; if they fold their arms or turn away, the dog could perceive it as a sign to back off. This responsiveness to physical cues likely developed over millennia, as dogs adapted to human communication styles.

Scent is yet another powerful medium through which dogs "understand" us. With up to 300 million olfactory receptors (compared to the six million in humans), a dog's sense of smell is capable of discerning emotions and even detecting illnesses. When humans experience stress or fear, their bodies release unique chemicals through sweat, which dogs can detect. "To a dog, every emotion has a scent," explains biologist Bruce Fogle, emphasizing that a dog's world is layered with aromatic information (Fogle, 2007).

In this way, dogs form a multidimensional understanding of humans, incorporating sound, sight, and scent into a holistic interpretation of our moods and intentions. The result is an astonishingly nuanced connection, where dogs often know what we need without our having to say a word.

Exploring Theories from ESP to Flock Behavior

The idea of "extra-sensory perception" (ESP) has captured the human imagination for decades. Though often relegated to the realm of the paranormal, ESP describes an ability to gather information beyond ordinary sensory channels. Interestingly, ESP may also serve as a metaphor for understanding the intuitive bonds that dogs seem to form with us.

Dogs have been observed to exhibit what many consider a form of ESP, especially when they anticipate their owners' arrival or seem to know when something is wrong. Rupert Sheldrake, a British biologist, documented countless accounts of animals "knowing" when their owners were coming home, a phenomenon he called "morphic resonance" (Sheldrake, 1999).
Sheldrake's controversial theory suggests that animals and humans are connected by fields of information, which allow them to communicate across space and time.

While some researchers remain skeptical of Sheldrake's work, the study of animal behavior in groups lends credibility to the idea that certain animals—including dogs—are wired to move and act as one. The study of flocking birds and schooling fish reveals an elegant example of non- verbal coordination. Without any obvious signaling, these animals react as a unit, seamlessly shifting directions as if guided by a shared consciousness. Scientists hypothesize that this phenomenon is enabled by both highly attuned sensory perception and an inherent drive for synchronicity, likely shaped by evolution as a survival mechanism (Couzin et al., 2005).

For dog owners, these insights suggest that dogs may have retained some capacity for this "group mind." It's possible that, when attuned closely to a human, a dog can sense their emotional state, physical health, and intentions. Whether or not we label it "telepathy," the communication that occurs is undeniably real, an interaction shaped by signals we may not even be aware we're sending

Non-Verbal Communication in the Animal Kingdom: Dogs, Horses, and Beyond

Understanding our dogs' communication style requires an appreciation for the broader realm of non-verbal communication in the animal kingdom. Horses, for example, display a remarkable sensitivity to human emotions. Equine-assisted therapy relies on a horse's natural capacity to sense and reflect human emotional states, which helps individuals work through psychological issues by observing how the horse responds to them. "Horses react to the slightest emotional shifts in humans," explains therapist Linda Kohanov, author of *The Tao of Equus* (Kohanov, 2001). This mirrors the way dogs attune to their owners' moods, using subtle cues to interpret how they should respond.

In a similar vein, recent research in animal behavior highlights how certain primates communicate complex ideas through gestures and expressions. Chimpanzees, for example, use over 66 distinct gestures to convey intentions, and many of these gestures are readily understood by humans, indicating a shared capacity for non-verbal interaction (Hobaiter et al., 2014). The parallels between dogs and primates suggest that non-verbal communication is deeply ingrained across species and serves as a foundational tool for bonding and survival.

Our dogs may not communicate in the same nuanced way as primates, yet their non-verbal signals—wagging tails, perked ears, tilted heads—speak volumes. These gestures may seem simple, but they reveal an intelligence that is profoundly social and adaptive, allowing dogs to communicate effectively with both other dogs and humans.

Dogs, through their behaviors and keen perceptions, offer us an opportunity to reconnect with forms of communication that transcend words. By tuning into these non-verbal cues, we engage in a kind of communion with them, one that feels almost mystical yet is grounded in biological and evolutionary science. Whether or not we ever fully understand the mechanisms, the connection itself is a gift, offering a glimpse into a world beyond language.

Chapter 3: Canine Intuition: Fact, Folklore, and Phenomea

From the tales of loyal hounds traveling miles to find their lost owners to accounts of dogs sensing impending earthquakes, the concept of a "sixth sense" in dogs has captured the human imagination for centuries. Yet, as enchanting as these stories are, they also prompt us to question: Are dogs truly equipped with a kind of intuition beyond our understanding? Or do we simply interpret their perceptive abilities as supernatural when they align so closely with our own emotions, intentions, or needs? In this chapter, we'll explore the science and folklore surrounding canine intuition, looking at everything from instinctual responses to potential evidence of phenomena beyond typical sensory experience.

Dog "Sixth Sense" Stories: Sensing Earthquakes, Illness, and Danger

Dogs are often attributed with an uncanny ability to sense changes in their environment. While some of these abilities are well-documented, others venture into more mysterious territory. For instance, numerous accounts emerged from the devastating Indian Ocean tsunami of 2004, describing how dogs, along with other animals, began behaving erratically hours before the disaster struck. It's believed that the animals sensed changes in ground vibrations or shifts in atmospheric pressure—sensory input far beyond human capacity but well within the realm of possibility for animals with such heightened senses.

In a similar vein, dogs have demonstrated an ability to detect illnesses in humans, particularly certain types of cancer. A study by Pine Street Foundation documented dogs identifying lung and breast cancer through smell with high accuracy, simply by sniffing patients' breath samples (McCulloch et al., 2006). Dogs have also been trained to alert people with diabetes when their blood sugar levels drop dangerously low, sensing the change through a shift in body odor. In these cases, the dog's response can be explained by its highly developed olfactory system, which includes

300 million scent receptors—compared to only six million in humans.

Yet, there are other cases that are harder to explain. Stories of dogs sensing an owner's impending arrival or displaying distress before an accident or sudden illness suggest that dogs may be able to "tune in" to something less tangible. Rupert Sheldrake, a biologist and author of *Dogs That Know When Their Owners Are Coming Home*, conducted experiments demonstrating that dogs would go to the door or window around the time their owners were about to return home, even without any other cues (Sheldrake, 1999). Though this remains controversial, Sheldrake's work inspires consideration of a shared, perhaps invisible, connection between dogs and humans.

Studies and Skepticism: Science on Animal Intuition

Despite the abundant anecdotes, scientific scrutiny is often skeptical of the idea that animals possess a "sixth sense." Psychologists and animal behaviorists argue that what seems like an extraordinary ability is often a product of associative learning and acute observational skills honed over centuries of domestication.

For instance, dogs are highly responsive to routine and small environmental cues. They learn, over time, that certain sounds, smells, or sights mean certain events are about to happen. A door closing in the distance might signify an owner's return, or the sound of a specific vehicle might prompt them to go to the window. Psychologists suggest that, in many cases, these behaviors reflect conditioned responses rather than intuitive knowledge.

That said, research into animal cognition and sensory capabilities has increasingly opened the door to possibilities beyond traditional explanations. For example, studies have found that some animals, such as homing pigeons, use the earth's magnetic fields to navigate. Dogs, too, have been shown to sense magnetic fields to a degree, and they appear to align themselves with the Earth's magnetic axis while urinating or defecating, a behavior documented in a study by Czech and German researchers (Hart et al., 2013).

Real-Life Anecdotes of Dogs Who "Just Know"

Beyond studies and skepticism, the real intrigue lies in the multitude of personal stories told by dog owners, stories that illustrate moments when their dogs seem to perceive things that we cannot. One well-known example is that of Hachiko, a Japanese Akita who famously waited at a train station every day for nearly ten years after his owner's death, seemingly aware on some level that his owner would not return. Hachiko's story resonates deeply with people worldwide, symbolizing both loyalty and an inexplicable depth of understanding.

Such stories often spark a sense of recognition among dog owners, who may remember similar, albeit less dramatic, moments with their own pets. My own family experienced something remarkable when our dog ran away and became lost for several days. In a surprising twist, my grandmother dreamed of the dog being in a forest, associated with something to do with a "star." Shortly after sharing her dream, we received a call from a forest ranger at a place called "The North Star" in a distant forest. He had found our dog, mirroring my grandmother's vision almost exactly.

Even if these experiences remain anecdotal, they underscore a remarkable connection that dog owners have long sensed and treasured. It could be that dogs, in attuning to us so closely, come to share our lives, our rhythms, and, sometimes, even our premonitions.

The Intrigue of the Unknown

So, where does all of this leave us? Do dogs truly have a sixth sense, or are they simply experts at reading our unspoken cues? The answer may lie somewhere in between, with a nod to both their sensory prowess and an affinity for forming bonds that go beyond the physical. Carl Jung, the Swiss psychologist, famously proposed the concept of a "collective unconscious," a shared human experience that links individuals through archetypal knowledge. Perhaps in our partnerships with dogs, this unconscious world opens up a little wider, allowing us both to step into an expanded realm of awareness and empathy.

While science may continue to explore and debate these phenomena, we need not wait for definitive answers to appreciate the remarkable relationship we have with our dogs. After all, as Antoine de Saint-Exupéry wrote in The Little Prince, "One sees clearly only with the heart.
Anything essential is invisible to the eyes." For dog owners, that invisible connection—the intuitive bond—is one of the most cherished aspects of living alongside our four-legged friends.

Fun Fact:

Studies have shown that many dog owners report a sense of "knowing" when their dogs need them or vice versa. This uncanny synchronicity is sometimes called "dog telepathy." In one famous study by biologist Rupert Sheldrake, dogs seemed to anticipate when their owners would return home—sometimes at unpredictable hours and without other cues like car sounds. Sheldrake proposed that this connection might be a type of telepathy or "morphic resonance," an unexplained bond that science is still puzzling over. It makes you wonder: how much are our dogs tuning into our thoughts?

Fun Fact:

Dogs can sense when we're looking at them—even if they can't see our eyes! Research has shown that dogs often respond to our gaze or mental focus, sometimes changing their behavior based on whether we're paying attention. This awareness is believed to be a combination of keen observation and a deep bond with us. So next time you "send" a thought to your dog, you might be surprised—your dog could be more tuned in than you think!

Fun Fact:

Did you know that some trainers use "remote influencing" techniques, where they mentally picture a dog responding to a command before giving it verbally? This practice stems from the idea that our dogs might pick up on subtle cues or even a bit of "thought energy" when we focus intently. While not scientifically proven, trainers have reported surprising success using visualization techniques to gently guide dogs without any physical signals—just a mental image and trust in the connection!

Chapter Four: The Role of Evolution in Canine Communication

The communication skills of dogs, refined and shaped over millennia, reveal more than an adaptation to human companionship—they highlight an intricate dance between natural selection and environmental influence. How did dogs come to understand human gestures, emotions, and even unspoken intentions so well? To answer this, we must look to their evolutionary roots, tracing back to a shared ancestry with wolves and the many adaptations that have enabled dogs to become deeply attuned to human life.

Wolves to Domesticated Dogs: Evolutionary Benefits of Understanding Humans

To appreciate the extraordinary ability of dogs to interpret human behavior, it's essential to understand their origins as pack animals. As social predators, wolves evolved to rely on group coordination, collaboration, and keen sensitivity to the body language and vocalizations of their pack mates. These skills are vital for hunting, raising offspring, and ensuring survival in complex social structures.

About 20,000-40,000 years ago, some wolves ventured closer to human settlements, drawn by the lure of food scraps and safety from larger predators. In turn, humans benefited from the wolves' watchful presence, which likely alerted them to potential dangers and deterred threats. Over generations, a mutualistic relationship developed, with certain wolves evolving to be more tolerant and attentive to human behaviors and expressions, traits that made them less fearful and more companionable.

This evolution set the foundation for dogs to inherit traits from their wolf ancestors—such as social intelligence, sensitivity to group dynamics, and a strong drive to understand the intentions of others. As time passed, selective breeding amplified these traits, and dogs became more adept at interpreting human cues, a skill that has persisted and expanded in modern breeds (Morey, 2014).

Survival and Communication in Animal Packs and Human-Dog Bonds

In the wild, survival often depends on an animal's ability to interpret its environment quickly and accurately, especially within social groups. For wolves, this meant picking up on subtle cues from pack members, whether it was an invitation to play, a command to halt, or a warning to back down. This "social literacy" became ingrained in wolves, and later in dogs, fostering a set of skills that enabled dogs to excel in their interactions with humans.

Dogs are often referred to as "hyper-social" animals, reflecting their extraordinary capacity to read and respond to the subtle social cues of others. In a study by Hare and Tomasello (2005), dogs were found to be more skilled than even primates at understanding human gestures such as pointing. While chimpanzees struggled with this task, dogs, even without prior training, could follow a human pointing at an object—a testament to their evolved ability to interpret human intention.

In modern life, this ability manifests as an uncanny knack for bonding with people across a range of environments: from busy cities to remote farms, from therapy work in hospitals to guiding search-and-rescue missions. Dogs have proven not only able to survive within human societies but also to play diverse roles, demonstrating adaptive versatility shaped by thousands of years of co-evolution.

Real-Life Anecdotes of Dogs Who "Just Know"

As we delve into the connections between dogs and humans, we find intriguing evidence of dogs' responses to subtle, often subconscious cues. Dogs, much like humans, have mirror neurons—cells in the brain that fire both when they perform an action and when they observe the same action being performed by another. This system helps dogs intuitively respond to our emotions and intentions, and it forms the neurological basis for empathy, a trait often observed in the human-dog bond (Romero et al., 2013).

For example, many dog owners notice that their pets seem to "know" when they're feeling sad, anxious, or happy, even without obvious changes in their behavior. This empathetic response likely stems from both mirror neuron activity and a deep-seated evolutionary trait to bond closely with humans. Such connections not only make dogs exceptionally responsive to human emotions but also enable them to adjust their behavior accordingly—whether by offering comfort, showing excitement, or maintaining calm in stressful situations.

This subconscious attunement brings to mind psychologist Carl Jung's idea of the "collective unconscious," which suggests that certain experiences and instincts are shared across generations and species. Perhaps dogs, as close partners of humans, share an evolved sensitivity that allows them to tap into this intuitive knowledge, perceiving shifts in mood, stress, or even danger without needing explicit information.

Unseen Bonds and Everyday Observations

For centuries, humans have marveled at the ways in which dogs seem to "know" things—often before we do. Whether sensing an approaching thunderstorm or reacting to the presence of an unfamiliar person, dogs demonstrate a range of behaviors that seem to tap into invisible signals in the environment. In some cases, their heightened awareness serves as an early-warning system, protecting both themselves and their human companions.

In my own experience, I remember hearing the faint sound of children's feet on the living room's polished wooden floor late at night. While it's possible that I was in a half-dream state, every time I awoke, my dog would already be alert, its ears perked, watching the room with a calm, quiet attentiveness. We both seemed to be drawn to something intangible, yet undeniably present. Such moments may be open to interpretation, but they emphasize the quiet, mysterious ways in which dogs and humans share space, picking up on cues that transcend the physical.

The Evolutionary Edge: Dogs' Communication with Humans as an Adaptive Advantage

Ultimately, dogs' deep connection to humans has evolved into one of their most valuable survival tools. Beyond physical attributes or hunting skills, it is the ability to interpret and adapt to human behavior that has made dogs successful in such a wide range of environments. This attunement not only strengthens the bond between dogs and humans but also allows dogs to excel in roles that require empathy, understanding, and adaptability.

In his book *The Other End of the Leash*, animal behaviorist Patricia McConnell suggests that our relationship with dogs may be one of the purest forms of interspecies connection, a partnership built on shared understanding and mutual respect (McConnell, 2002). This connection likely confers evolutionary advantages for both parties—humans benefit from dogs' protection, companionship, and unique sensory skills, while dogs gain shelter, food, and care in return.

In the next chapter, we'll explore how we can tap into these bonds more intentionally, using mindfulness and non-verbal cues to foster a deeper connection with our dogs. The journey of co-evolution has given us more than just a loyal companion; it has offered us a mirror through which we can learn more about ourselves and our shared instincts.

Chapter Five: Non-Verbal Cues in Training and Daily Life

Tuning into Your Dog's Subtle Signals

Non-verbal communication is a fundamental part of how we interact with our dogs—whether we realize it or not. For dogs, body language, facial expressions, and subtle shifts in energy are essential for interpreting the world around them. By tuning into these cues ourselves, we open a path to deeper understanding and connection. This chapter explores practical ways to become more mindful of our non-verbal cues, creating a communication style that enhances training and strengthens the bond with our dogs.

Dogs are masters at picking up on physical cues. They notice everything: the way we hold our bodies, the tension in our muscles, and even the smallest flicker of emotion on our faces. As animal cognition researcher Alexandra Horowitz points out, dogs are "keen observers of the physical manifestations of our internal states" (Horowitz, 2009). This sensitivity is part of what makes them such intuitive companions, often responding to our feelings before we're even fully aware of them ourselves.

Learning to tune into our dog's signals requires us to pause and observe their responses in different situations. For example, a tail wag is generally a sign of friendliness or excitement, but the pace and height of the wag can offer more nuanced information. A low, slow wag might signal uncertainty, while a high, fast wag could indicate excitement or agitation. Similarly, a dog's body posture—whether it's relaxed, rigid, or low to the ground—provides insight into how they're feeling and how they may react.

One of the simplest ways to start paying closer attention to your dog's signals is through observation exercises. Spend a few moments each day observing your dog in various states: at rest, during play, and in new or stimulating environments. Notice how their body language shifts and how they respond to you without verbal direction. Through these observations, you'll gain insight into their unique communication style and learn to recognize subtle shifts that might otherwise go unnoticed.

Mindfulness and Presence with Your Dog

Being present is key to effective non-verbal communication. Dogs live in the moment, making them attuned to the immediate energy of their surroundings. When we bring a mindful presence into our interactions with them, we align with their natural way of being, making it easier for them to understand our intentions and for us to interpret their responses.

Mindfulness practices, even something as simple as taking a few deep breaths before engaging with your dog, can improve the clarity of your interactions. This approach also helps us become more aware of our internal states. Our dogs pick up on our stress, excitement, or calm, and they mirror these emotions back to us. By centering ourselves, we can project a calm, reassuring energy that positively influences our dog's behavior.

Consider incorporating short mindfulness exercises into your daily routine with your dog. For instance, during a walk, practice focusing entirely on the experience: the sounds, sights, and smells around you, as well as your dog's reactions. Notice how your dog's energy shifts and how they respond to your calm focus. This mindful connection fosters a natural synchronization, helping your dog feel more secure and allowing you to communicate more effectively.

Techniques for "Silent Training" and Enhancing Mutual Understanding

Silent training involves guiding your dog through non-verbal cues, relying on gestures, eye contact, and body language instead of spoken commands. This technique builds on dogs' natural inclination to read our physical signals and helps develop a subtle, intuitive communication style that both you and your dog can enjoy.

For instance, instead of saying "sit," you might use a hand gesture, slowly raising your hand as you guide your dog into the sitting position. Over time, your dog will learn to associate this gesture with the desired action. This approach can be used for a range of commands, from "stay" to "come." Once the non-verbal cue is established, you'll find that your dog often responds more readily, as they're attuned to the physical rather than the verbal.

Eye contact is another powerful tool in silent training. Dogs interpret eye contact as a form of communication, and a steady, gentle gaze can serve as a signal for calm or encouragement. For example, if your dog seems anxious, holding a calm, reassuring gaze can help ease their tension. Likewise, breaking eye contact at the right moment—such as when they start barking or jumping—can communicate that the behavior is undesirable.

Incorporating silent training doesn't mean you need to abandon spoken commands altogether; rather, it's about enhancing your communication toolkit. Using both verbal and non-verbal cues interchangeably creates a well-rounded language that can help reduce misunderstandings and strengthen your dog's responsiveness.

Listening to Each Other: The Feedback Loop of Non-Verbal Communication
A successful communication exchange is a two-way street. Just as we strive to understand our dog's body language and energy, they're constantly reading ours. Dogs naturally create a feedback loop, adjusting their responses based on the cues they receive from us. This reciprocal understanding can be cultivated intentionally, creating an even stronger bond over time.

To establish this feedback loop, make it a habit to respond to your dog's cues with conscious adjustments in your own behavior. If you notice that they're hesitating or seem uncertain, try softening your posture or slowing down your movements. Alternatively, if they're excited and playful, match their energy with open, inviting gestures. Over time, this exchange creates a mutual language in which you and your dog respond to each other's signals intuitively.

This approach also applies to moments of discipline or correction. When correcting a behavior, maintain calm, controlled body language and avoid excessive gestures that might escalate the situation. The goal is to model the behavior you want them to mirror.

As animal trainer Ken Ramirez notes, "Communication with animals is about mutual understanding, not dominance or control" (Ramirez, 2019).

By being attuned to this feedback loop, we learn to communicate more thoughtfully and respectfully with our dogs, fostering a sense of partnership rather than hierarchy.

Non-Verbal Communication in Daily Routines

Beyond training, non-verbal cues are at play in everyday routines, from mealtime rituals to bedtime routines. Dogs quickly pick up on these routines and often begin anticipating our actions. For instance, the simple act of picking up your dog's leash is a non-verbal cue that signals the start of a walk, prompting an excited response. Similarly, setting a bowl down might trigger a "sit" or "wait" response if this has been incorporated into your mealtime routine.

Using these daily routines as training moments reinforces your non-verbal communication. By being intentional with your actions, you create opportunities for your dog to learn and respond without spoken commands. Each routine becomes an exercise in understanding, building trust and predictability.

In these moments, the boundary between training and daily life blurs. Every interaction becomes an opportunity to reinforce understanding and build mutual respect. Through mindful presence and consistent routines, you can create a communication style that's as natural as it is effective.

A Shared Language: Bonding Beyond Words

The beauty of non-verbal communication lies in its subtlety and depth. For both you and your dog, building a shared language rooted in gestures, eye contact, and energy brings new dimensions to your relationship. In a way, it allows you to tap into a kind of intuitive connection that mirrors the natural, unspoken bonds found in animal packs and human relationships.

By learning to communicate silently, you and your dog develop a language all your own—one that's felt as much as it's seen. This language of silent signals, shared experiences, and mutual responsiveness doesn't just create an obedient dog; it fosters a loyal, intuitive companion who understands and trusts you in ways that transcend spoken words.

In the next chapter, we'll explore the role of energy and emotion in this unique language. From how dogs sense and respond to our moods to ways we can cultivate calm, positive energy, we'll dive into the power of emotional presence as a cornerstone of dog-human communication.

Chapter Six: The Power of Energy and Emotion in Communication

If there's one thing every dog owner knows, it's that our emotions don't go unnoticed. Dogs have an incredible capacity for sensing how we feel, often responding with empathy, excitement, or calmness based on our mood. But how can we harness this connection? And, more importantly, how can we learn to project the right energy when we want to communicate effectively? In this chapter, we explore the role of emotion and energy in non-verbal communication, focusing on the power of emotional presence and "sending" as a way to build trust, reduce stress, and foster a harmonious relationship with your dog.

Can Dogs Sense Our Emotions? Science and Stories

The idea that dogs can sense human emotions might feel instinctively true, but it's also backed by scientific findings. Studies show that dogs are exceptionally attuned to human faces and vocal tones, which they use to gauge our emotional states. In one fascinating experiment conducted at the University of Helsinki, researchers found that dogs could distinguish between happy and angry human faces with remarkable accuracy (Racca et al., 2012). This ability to interpret human emotions is likely a product of domestication; over thousands of years, dogs evolved to become adept at reading human social cues as part of their survival strategy.

The presence of mirror neurons in dogs, similar to those in humans, may further explain their sensitivity. Mirror neurons are brain cells that activate both when an animal performs an action and when it observes the same action in another being. This capacity for empathy and attunement, some scientists suggest, allows dogs to mirror our emotions, effectively "feeling" what we feel. As a result, a calm human tends to inspire a calm dog, while stress or anxiety can lead to nervousness or agitation in our pets.

Anecdotes of dogs providing comfort during moments of sadness, excitement during times of celebration, or protection in situations of perceived threat are plentiful. These stories reinforce what science is only beginning to understand: dogs can read and respond to our emotional energy. With this knowledge, we can intentionally cultivate an energy that supports both our dog's well-being and our own.

Using Calm and Positive Energy in Training

Energy and emotion are at the heart of effective training. Dogs are incredibly sensitive to the vibes we bring into each interaction, and they often respond to the emotional tone we set rather than the specific command we give. This is especially true for anxious or reactive dogs, who rely on their owners' calm and steady presence as an anchor.

To create a supportive energy for training, start by focusing on your breathing. Before issuing a command or beginning an exercise, take a deep breath and center yourself. When you project calmness, your dog picks up on that energy and feels safer, which helps them relax and focus. Likewise, if you're trying to encourage excitement or enthusiasm, bring an upbeat, open posture and tone into the interaction. Your dog will mirror these emotions, making them more responsive and engaged.

It can be helpful to visualize the kind of energy you want to communicate. Picture yourself as a calm, steady presence, or as an encouraging and positive guide. As you project this visualization, your dog will sense the shift in your energy, responding naturally. Many trainers describe this process as "sending"—a technique that involves mentally projecting an image or feeling that aligns with your goal. For example, if you want your dog to follow you calmly, visualize yourself as grounded and in control. If you want them to come running to you with enthusiasm, visualize warmth and excitement.

Exercises to Cultivate Mindful Energy Exchange

Building a connection rooted in energy exchange isn't just a concept; it's a practice. These exercises are designed to help you cultivate the mindful presence that enhances communication with your dog. Trust the process, even if it feels unusual at first; over time, both you and your dog will benefit from this heightened awareness.

Exercise 1: The "Grounding Breath"

1. Begin in a quiet space with your dog by your side. Sit comfortably and close your eyes.
2. Take three slow, deep breaths, letting each exhale ground you further. Imagine that each breath releases tension, leaving only calmness.
3. Picture yourself as a source of calm, steady energy. Visualize this calmness radiating outwards, filling the space around you.
4. Open your eyes and observe your dog. Notice any changes in their demeanor. Often, dogs will settle or lie down as they pick up on your calm energy.

This grounding breath exercise helps prepare both you and your dog for a relaxed, focused interaction. Practicing this exercise before a walk or training session can set a tone of mutual calm.

Exercise 2: Visualize and "Send" Your Intention

1. Think of a specific action you'd like your dog to take, such as sitting or staying close to you.
2. Close your eyes and picture your dog performing this action. Imagine how they look, how they feel, and the energy they emit when they're focused and calm.
3. Open your eyes and project this mental image to your dog. If they respond, reinforce it with a gentle "good" or a treat to encourage their engagement with your energy.

This exercise taps into the concept of sending—a technique that is part visualization, part intention. Dogs often respond to these non-verbal cues, especially when they are accustomed to your focused, mindful presence.

Projecting Calm in Moments of Stress

When our dogs are stressed or anxious, they look to us for reassurance. In these moments, the energy we project becomes especially important. Our dogs need us to be a steady anchor, someone they can rely on to keep them safe.

One way to project calm is through the "open stance" technique:

1.	Stand with your feet shoulder-width apart, arms relaxed at your sides, and breathe slowly and deeply.
2.	Soften your gaze and maintain a neutral expression. Avoid leaning over your dog, which can come across as confrontational.
3.	Imagine a calm, grounding energy flowing from your center to your surroundings. Let your dog sense this energy without directing it at them.

With practice, this technique becomes a natural way to convey calmness. Over time, your dog will learn to associate your steady presence with safety, reducing their stress response.

Trusting the Process of "Sending"

"Sending" is a concept rooted in intention and belief—an approach that can feel foreign at first, but yields remarkable results with time. At its core, sending isn't about control; it's about projecting your intention calmly and confidently, trusting that your dog can sense it.

One of the most significant aspects of sending is learning to let go of the need to understand exactly *how* it works. As much as we might want scientific proof, some things in the dog- human bond transcend immediate explanation. Think of sending as a subtle art, like creating harmony through music. You can't always pinpoint the exact mechanism, but you can feel it working.

Dogs respond to our intention because they live in a world where energy and instinct take precedence. Trust that by sending an image, feeling, or thought, you're speaking to a part of your dog that doesn't require words. With time, both you and your dog will become more attuned to this shared language.

Spillover Benefits: How Working with Energy Enhances Your Life

The benefits of developing a mindful, energy-centered relationship with your dog extend far beyond training sessions. By cultivating calmness, presence, and intention in your interactions, you'll notice a natural increase in self-awareness and emotional control in all areas of life. This approach to communication encourages you to become more mindful of your own energy, making it easier to manage stress, enhance focus, and maintain emotional balance.

Working with energy and intention builds resilience and teaches patience—a lesson our dogs often remind us of daily. As you and your dog deepen your connection through mindful practices, you may find that other relationships, whether personal or professional, benefit from the same attentiveness and calm presence.

The Shared Journey

Developing an understanding of energy and emotion with your dog is a journey of exploration and growth. It's not a quick fix or a shortcut to obedience; rather, it's a path toward creating a bond that's rooted in empathy and mutual respect. Trust that your dog responds to the energy you project, and with time, this shared understanding will become one of the most rewarding aspects of your relationship.

In the next chapter, we'll take this journey deeper, focusing on visualization and "sending" as an intuitive communication method. By learning how to guide your dog's behavior through mental imagery, you'll open new doors to connection and trust, enriching both your lives in ways you might not have imagined.

Chapter Seven: Visualization and "Sending": Communication Without Words

As we deepen our exploration into canine communication, we arrive at one of the most intriguing methods: visualization and "sending." This chapter unpacks how we can use mental imagery and focused intention to connect with our dogs on a deeper, intuitive level.

Visualization isn't simply a tool for obedience or training but a way of sharing a mental space with our dogs, creating a sense of shared purpose and understanding. While it's difficult to define the "how" of sending in purely scientific terms, many handlers, trainers, and dog owners have found success using these methods. Here, we explore both the art and science behind it.

The Power of Mental Imagery

The mind's capacity for imagery is powerful. Visualization engages not only our cognitive functions but also our emotional and physiological responses. Studies in sports psychology show that athletes who visualize their movements with precision perform better, indicating that our mental images influence our physical actions (Moran, 2004). While dogs may not "see" our images directly, they are perceptive to the intent and energy behind our focus, often responding with attuned behavior.

When we hold a clear image of what we want our dogs to do—whether it's running to our side or waiting calmly—they can sense that intention. Visualization becomes a form of non-verbal guidance. In essence, it's like giving your dog a silent "map" of what you're hoping they'll do.

Visualization allows for a richer, layered form of communication, one that operates on levels beyond voice commands or hand signals.

Techniques to "Send" Thoughts and Intentions

Learning to send thoughts and intentions requires both practice and patience. Unlike traditional training techniques, it's less about consistency of command and more about clarity of mind.

Below are methods to cultivate your sending abilities, each building on mindfulness, focus, and trust in your connection with your dog.

1. Create a Clear Mental Image

Think about the action you want your dog to take. Imagine them performing this action in detail. Picture their posture, their movement, and even the emotions you want them to feel. Hold this image in your mind and feel it as if it were happening in the present.

For example, if you want your dog to walk calmly at your side, visualize them moving with an easy, relaxed stride, close to you. Imagine yourself feeling calm and in control, radiating that confidence. Your dog will pick up on this energy, associating it with the visual message you're sending.

2. "Broadcast" Your Intention

Once you've created a mental image, the next step is to mentally "send" it. Picture this thought or image traveling from you to your dog. Hold the intention lightly, without pushing or straining. Imagine it as an invitation rather than a demand. Visualizing your intention with an open heart allows your dog to receive it in a non-threatening way, reinforcing the bond of trust between you.

3. Practice with Simple Commands

Start with simple actions that your dog already understands, such as sitting or lying down. Visualize the action and mentally send it to your dog without using words. Observe their reaction. This practice not only builds your visualization skills but also strengthens your dog's ability to tune into your mental cues.

Over time, as your dog grows accustomed to receiving your silent cues, you'll find that they respond with increased accuracy, often acting without the need for spoken commands.

Successful Examples in Training: Connecting Through Imagery

Many dog trainers and handlers have found visualization to be a powerful addition to traditional training. One story from a respected dog trainer illustrates the effectiveness of this technique in high-stress environments. During an agility competition, a handler used visualization to calm her dog, who was visibly anxious and distracted. She closed her eyes and imagined her dog performing the course with confidence and focus. The dog visibly settled, tuning into her owner's energy, and successfully completed the course. While the effect of visualization isn't fully understood, stories like these suggest a strong link between a handler's mental state and a dog's behavior.

Real-Life Anecdote

One family recalls their experience when training their dog to stay close in busy public spaces. Whenever they would take walks downtown, they would first spend a few quiet moments together. Each family member would visualize the dog walking calmly at their side, resisting the temptation to pull on the leash or get distracted. With time, this practice seemed to anchor the dog, who began to naturally fall into step and stay focused even in bustling environments. For the family, the act of visualization became a shared ritual, something that reinforced their bond and added an element of calm to their outings.

Balancing Intuition with Training Tools

Visualization and sending are not meant to replace traditional training methods but to enhance them. Think of them as an additional layer of communication that bridges the gap between physical commands and intuitive understanding. Dogs trained with both physical commands and visualized intentions often exhibit a more nuanced response to their handlers.

It's also important to balance intuition with training tools for clarity and consistency. Visualization is most effective when paired with training foundations that your dog already understands. Rather than expecting your dog to grasp entirely new concepts through visualization alone, use it to reinforce behaviors they've already learned, deepening their comprehension and willingness.

The Value of Practice and Patience

Like any skill, sending and visualization require consistent practice. Don't be discouraged if your dog doesn't respond immediately. Remember that even slight changes in behavior, such as increased focus or calmness, are signs that your connection is strengthening. As you practice, your ability to send clear, intentional thoughts will improve, and your dog's responsiveness will grow.

The patience required for this method is part of its beauty. In a world that often demands instant results, the act of slowing down and connecting with your dog through visualization brings a peaceful rhythm to training. Both you and your dog will benefit from the mindful approach, which fosters an environment of mutual respect and understanding.

Visualization Exercises to Deepen Your Connection

These exercises will help you refine your sending skills and enhance your dog's responsiveness.

Exercise 1: "Picture the Path"

1. Begin by choosing a goal for your walk, such as a calm pace with minimal distractions.
2. Close your eyes and visualize yourself and your dog walking harmoniously. Imagine the sights, sounds, and feelings you expect.
3. Hold this image as you begin the walk, periodically returning to it if your dog gets distracted.
4. Notice your dog's responses and reward them for staying close or walking calmly.

This exercise is particularly useful for working with dogs who get easily distracted. It helps reinforce a shared mental path, creating a sense of teamwork.

Exercise 2: Projecting Calm at the Vet's Office

Vet visits can be stressful for both dogs and owners. Before your appointment, take a few moments to sit quietly with your dog.

1. Close your eyes and visualize the waiting room, picturing yourself and your dog sitting calmly together.
2. See your dog relaxed and at ease, receiving attention from the vet calmly.
3. Send a steadying, reassuring energy, reminding yourself that you are your dog's anchor.

This practice can help your dog feel more secure in potentially stressful settings, as they will sense your calm and draw strength from it.

Leaving Room for Mystery

When we engage in sending and visualization, we enter a realm of connection that doesn't rely on strict scientific validation. Some experiences defy explanation, existing in the subtle space between evidence and intuition. Think of Antoine de Saint-Exupéry's words in *The Little Prince*: "One sees clearly only with the heart. What is essential is invisible to the eye." Dogs, in their openness to our intentions, teach us to trust our hearts as much as our minds.

Even if we don't fully understand how visualization affects our dogs, the impact is real. It reminds us of the unspoken bond that draws humans and dogs together, and how much we can learn by simply observing, feeling, and trusting the connection.

In the next chapter, we'll explore the remarkable ways dogs have acted as guides, healers, and partners in human lives. From therapy work to search-and-rescue missions, we'll delve into stories and studies showing the incredible support dogs offer when they pick up on our needs and respond with their unique "sixth sense."

Chapter Eight: Dogs in Human Lives: Guardians, Healers, and Partners

Since their domestication thousands of years ago, dogs have become woven into the fabric of human lives in profound ways. They are far more than mere companions; dogs hold roles as protectors, emotional supports, and sometimes even life-savers. Their heightened instincts and intuition often allow them to sense subtle shifts in the environment and in human emotions, leading to incredible acts of assistance and even heroism. For centuries, stories about these abilities have captured our imaginations and cemented dogs' role as cherished family members and partners in life.

Guardians in Times of Crisis

The most heroic stories of dogs often emerge during disasters when their skills are tested under extreme conditions. Search-and-rescue dogs, specifically trained to locate survivors after natural disasters, exhibit a unique combination of resilience, sensitivity, and drive. In Turkey, following the devastating 1999 İzmit earthquake, a creative solution was devised to maintain dogs' morale and motivation as the days wore on. With fewer survivors found over time, handlers started hiding themselves under rubble, allowing their dogs to experience the reward of a successful "find" when spirits were flagging. This technique proved invaluable in sustaining the dogs' determination and illustrates how these animals thrive on purpose and connection with humans, responding to emotional cues from their handlers just as strongly as they respond to scent cuesances, such as the aftermath of the 2011 earthquake and tsunami in Japan, search-and-rescue dogs were able to locate trapped individuals amidst chaotic environments, showcasing their ability to cut through overwhelming sensory input and focus on their task. Studies have shown that trained SAR dogs can differentiate between living and deceased persons and prioritize the scent of survivors. This capability—likely rooted in their extraordinary olfactory senses—is often paired with dogs' unique sensitivity to human body language and emotion, making them indispensable partners during disasters.

Healers in Life

The healing power of dogs extends far beyond rescue missions; in everyday life, they serve as therapeutic partners for people of all ages and backgrounds. Numerous studies have validated what dog owners have known intuitively: the presence of a dog can reduce stress, alleviate symptoms of depression, and improve cardiovascular health. A study published by the American Heart Association found that dog ownership is associated with a 33% reduced risk of death for heart attack survivors living alone . This association is linked to physical activity dogs encourage through regular walks, along with the reduction in stress hormones facilitated by pet interaction.

Therapy dogs are increasingly found in hospitals, nursing homes, and rehabilitation centers, providing comfort and joy to patients experiencing pain, isolation, or recovery. In a study by the Mayo Clinic, researchers found that just 12 minutes of interaction with a therapy dog can significantly lower pain levels in fibromyalgia patients . Children facing long-term hospital stays as veterans with PTSD, often show immediate improvements in mood and outlook after sessions with therapy dogs. These experiences underscore how dogs can sense and adapt to human emotional states, creating non-verbal connections that science is only beginning to understand.

Extraordinary Senses and the "Sixth Sense"

Dogs' sensory abilities far surpass our own in many respects, with their hearing, smell, and even vision finely attuned to pick up on details humans may miss. A dog's sense of smell, for example, is estimated to be between 10,000 and 100,000 times more acute than a human's. This capacity allows them to detect volatile organic compounds that signal illnesses like cancer and diabetes. In a 2006 study published in *Integrative Cancer Therapies*, researchers trained dogs to detect breast and lung

cancer with 88% accuracy simply by sniffing patients' breath samples .
This has opened doors for further research iogs as diagnostic aids, particularly in cases where early detection is critical.

Furthermore, dogs seem to possess a kind of "sixth sense" that enables them to perceive changes in the human body and emotional state, often before these shifts become visible to others. In earthquake-prone regions, anecdotal evidence has long suggested that dogs can detect seismic activity before humans notice any tremors.

Although this remains speculative, scientists hypothesize that dogs may be responding to subtle ground vibrations or shifts in atmospheric pressure. Following the 2004 tsunami in Southeast Asia, there were reports of dogs that had behaved unusually—whining, refusing to go outdoors, and even running inland—just hours before the disaster struck. This behavior points to an awareness of environmental cues that is beyond human perception.

Partners in Emotional Resilience

For many people, dogs play an irreplaceable role in their emotional lives. Dogs have an extraordinary ability to read and respond to human emotions, often providing support during times of grief, stress, or loneliness. This ability is especially significant for individuals who may struggle with anxiety or depression. Therapy and service dogs are trained to detect physiological signs of an oncoming panic attack, such as changes in body temperature or scent, and respond by providing calming pressure or alerting their handlers. These dogs offer a unique form of intervention that enhances both the mental and physical well-being of their human partners.

One moving example of this is seen in the use of therapy dogs rehabilitation programs. Many veterans describe how their service dogs not only assist them in daily tasks but also provide a grounding presence that helps mitigate PTSD symptoms. One veteran shared that his service dog would sense his elevated stress levels before he could consciously recognize them, helping him avoid situations that could trigger a flashback. Research on these interventions suggests that the companionship and stability dogs provide can significantly improve quality of life and emotional resilience.

Embracing the Mystery of Canine Instincts

While we may not fulls of dogs' sensory capabilities or their attunement to our emotions, it is clear that their presence has profound impacts on our lives. As guardians, healers, and partners, they offer protection, unconditional love, and resilience in a way that transcends explanation.
This chapter invites us to honor and nurture these remarkable qualities, recognizing that the science behind them may one day catch up with what dog lovers have long felt to be true: that dogs are uniquely gifted companions who bridge worlds both seen and unseen.

Dogs have always been extraordinary in their roles, not only as physical protectors but as emotional and spiritual guides. Their lives remind us of virtues such as loyalty, joy, and an almost otherworldly sensitivity to their environment. Just as Saint-Exupéry wrote in *The Little Prince*, "It is only with the heart that one can see rightly; what is essential is invisible to the eye," so too do dogs seem to "see" with their hearts. They move through the world with an innate trust in their senses, encouraging us to cultivate our own instincts and intuition, qualities we may have let grow dormant over time.

A Source of Unconditional Love and Understanding

Dogs possess an innate understanding of what humans need emotionally, offering companionship that's both steady and restorative. This capacity for connection has led some to call them "angels without wings." They sense when we are in distress, and without hesitation, they are there with gentle eyes, a calming presence, or a paw on our hand. Many studies now back up what dog lovers have always known intuitively: a dog's presence can lift our spirits, relieve stress, and even slow the heart rate, offering a type of therapy that few human interactions can replicate.

In one study conducted by Azabu University in Japan, scientists found that when owners and their dogs gaze into each other's eyes, both release the "love hormone" oxytocin, creating a feedback loop of affection that mimics the bond between a parent and child (Nagasawa et al., 2015). This deep connection is perhaps why dogs are so effective in emotional support roles, especially with children and individuals experiencing mental health challenges (Odendaal & Meintjes, 2003; Beetz et al., 2012).

Instincts and Sensing the Unseen

A key aspect of a dog's wisdom is its reliance on instinct. While we often second-guess ourselves, dogs act on their gut feelings, and they do so with conviction. This quality has sparked an entire field of study into animal behavior and intuition. Dogs are often able to perceive subtle changes in their surroundings or detect shifts in human physiology before they become apparent to us. For example, dogs can pick up on scent changes associated with stress or illness, and they respond in ways that suggest an awareness of things beyond our conscious perception.

This natural attunement to invisible cues has led to dogs being trained to detect illnesses like cancer, diabetes, and even epileptic seizures. When trained, dogs can identify specific volatile organic compounds emitted by diseased cells, a skill that can potentially save lives by prompting early diagnosis and treatment. They perform these feats of perception with an ease that humbles us, reminding us of the power and reliability of intuition.

A Teacher of Presence and Patience

If there's anything dogs can teach us, it's to embrace the present moment fully. Dogs do not dwell on yesterday's troubles or worry about tomorrow's challenges. They live in the here and now, responding to what's immediately before them. This mindfulness is something we, as dog owners, are privileged to witness and learn from. Spending time with a dog can remind us to slow down, observe, and find joy in the simple things—like a patch of sunlight on the floor or the rustling leaves in a park.

For humans, the practice of "sending"—transmitting thoughts and intentions to communicate with dogs—requires a similar kind of presence and attention. As we focus on connecting with our dogs on an unspoken level, we become more attuned to subtle cues, both within ourselves and in our environment. This practice not only strengthens our bond with our dogs but also sharpens our own intuition, encouraging us to trust the quiet, often-overlooked signals from our minds and bodies.

A Bridge Between Worlds

Dogs seem to exist in a liminal space, one foot in our world and one in another that we only faintly perceive. Stories abound of dogs alerting their owners to danger, seemingly sensing threats before they manifest. Some believe that this sensitivity allows dogs to serve as intermediaries between the physical and the spiritual realms. In folklore and literature, dogs are often portrayed as protectors against unseen forces and as guardians of thresholds between life and death. For example, in Greek mythology, Cerberus, the three-headed dog, guards the entrance to the underworld, a powerful symbol of a dog's role in protecting against the unknown.

In modern life, this quality of dogs is perhaps most poignantly seen in their work with terminally ill patients. Therapy dogs visiting hospices have been observed behaving differently around patients nearing the end of life, as if attuned to shifts that others cannot perceive. These quiet, gentle interactions offer comfort and companionship in a time of transition, embodying the grace that only animals seem to bring to life's most profound moments.

Cherishing the Mystery

In embracing all that dogs offer—protection, healing, companionship, and mystery—we open ourselves to a richer experience of life. It is through dogs that we can glimpse our own forgotten capacities for perception, trust, and love. They teach us to see beyond the visible, to trust in the unknown, and to honor the connections that surpass explanation. Perhaps it is not for us to fully understand these abilities but to accept and cherish them, knowing they bring immense value to our lives.

This chapter invites readers to pause and appreciate the wisdom inherent in their own dog's behaviors, to recognize that each bark, wag, and watchful glance carries layers of understanding that go beyond what we see on the surface. In doing so, we may come to view our canine companions not only as pets but as messengers, teachers, and steadfast friends who help us reconnect with our truest selves.

Chapter Nine: Insights from Psychology and Animal Behavior

Jungian Perspectives and the Collective Unconscious

Carl Jung's concept of the collective unconscious suggests that all living beings share a vast reservoir of memories, instincts, and archetypes—a set of universal templates embedded within us that shape behavior and perception. Jung believed that this collective unconscious connects all beings, forming a kind of spiritual blueprint for experiences across species (Jung, 1936). In essence, this connection provides each species, including dogs, with access to intrinsic knowledge and instinctual responses, as if drawing from an ancient, collective memory.

Jungian archetypes—such as the hero, caregiver, and wise elder—emerge from this collective unconscious, affecting our actions, relationships, and even our relationships with animals. For example, the archetype of the "protector" resonates deeply in the relationship between humans and dogs. Dogs, often perceived as guardians, seem to embody this archetype naturally, taking on roles that align with both human expectations and their instinctive behaviors. In dogs, we might see an immediate response to danger or a readiness to comfort—a "knowing" that transcends individual training and speaks to a shared, ancient role in their bond with humans.

The idea that animals tap into this collective pool of archetypal knowledge sheds light on why dogs may "just know" things about us, such as when we are sad or in need of comfort, even if we have not signaled it in any obvious way. By viewing canine intuition through the lens of Jung's theory, we might understand these behaviors not as isolated phenomena but as reflections of a universal wisdom that dogs and humans share, tapping into a common field of experience and understanding.

Synchronicity: Meaningful Coincidences and Shared Experiences

Jung's concept of synchronicity refers to events that are meaningfully related, despite lacking a clear cause-and-effect connection. Jung proposed that synchronicities arise when inner thoughts align with external events in ways that feel too significant to be mere coincidence (Jung, 1952). This phenomenon suggests a bridge between inner consciousness and external reality, a notion that resonates deeply with dog owners who've observed their pets responding intuitively to their emotions, thoughts, or even unspoken intentions.

One example of synchronicity with animals is seen in stories where dogs seem to anticipate their owner's arrival or sense an impending event. Such experiences might appear uncanny or telepathic to an outsider, but within Jung's framework, they can be understood as synchronous occurrences—moments where the inner experiences of one being (a human's need or emotional state) align with the external response of another (a dog's behavior or readiness to comfort).

This view allows us to interpret these encounters not as isolated incidents but as part of a larger web of interconnectedness that spans both psychological and physical realities.

Archetypes in Animal Behavior: Intuition, Instinct, and Empathy

The archetypes within the collective unconscious might help explain some of the profound behaviors and traits that define dogs. The "caregiver" archetype, often activated in times of distress or need, is one of the most potent symbols in human-canine interactions. Dogs may display this behavior instinctively, as though they have an innate blueprint guiding them to offer comfort and protection. This aligns with studies demonstrating how dogs are uniquely attuned to human emotions and social cues, often responding in ways that provide emotional support without any explicit training (Custance & Mayer, 2012).

In addition to the caregiver archetype, Jung's "shadow" archetype, which represents the unconscious mind's repressed aspects, might also surface in dogs. Dogs have been observed mirroring their owners' suppressed fears or anxieties, almost as if they reflect the parts of ourselves we are not fully aware of. For instance, a dog might develop nervous behaviors in response to an owner's unacknowledged stress, acting as a mirror to the owner's internal state. This perspective deepens our understanding of empathy and emotional attunement in dogs, highlighting how they not only detect but may also embody our unseen feelings.

A Shared Intuitive Field

A Shared Intuitive Field

Beyond individual traits or archetypes, Jung's ideas point to an underlying shared field of intuition that includes both animals and humans. In one memorable study by Sheldrake (1981), a large sample of dog owners reported their dogs acting noticeably different before they arrived home, regardless of the time of day or predictable routine. While science typically attributes this to conditioning or keen observational skills, the notion of a shared field of consciousness offers an alternative view. Perhaps dogs are connected to us in ways that elude current scientific understanding, picking up on signals transmitted through this shared unconscious field.

By acknowledging the possibility of such connections, we encourage an openness toward phenomena we might otherwise dismiss. While science has yet to provide concrete answers, stories of dogs anticipating owner arrivals, sensing danger, or mirroring emotions offer ample evidence that a bond exists—one that seems rooted in a field of awareness accessible to both dogs and humans.

While the exact mechanisms of our connection with dogs may remain mysterious, the emotional and intuitive resonance we share with them is something to honor and nurture.

By exploring the wisdom of the collective unconscious and synchronicity, we come closer to understanding the depth of our relationship with dogs. Their responses to us, whether rooted in instinct, archetypes, or intuition, remind us of the profound interconnectedness that binds all sentient beings—an interwoven consciousness that calls us to greater awareness, empathy, and mutual respect.

Chapter Ten: Exploring Skepticism -A Balanced Perspective

In our quest to understand canine intuition and seemingly telepathic connections, we must approach both open-mindedness and scientific rigor. Dogs have fascinated people for centuries with their uncanny abilities, from warning humans of impending seizures to sensing natural disasters. These remarkable traits inspire many to believe in a form of canine telepathy, yet science often challenges these perceptions, requiring evidence beyond anecdotes. By examining skepticism thoughtfully, we gain a more balanced appreciation of our dogs' exceptional abilities without dismissing possibilities outright.

The Limits of Scientific Inquiry and Animal Perception

At the heart of the debate around canine intuition is science's reliance on measurable evidence. While dogs' perceptive abilities are well-documented, some scientists attribute behaviors like "knowing" when an owner is returning or sensing emotional changes to conditioning and heightened sensory awareness. Studies like those by Clive Wynne and Monique Udell emphasize the extent of dogs' sensitivity to human emotions, often interpreting minor body language cues and responding intuitively (Udell et al., 2010). In these cases, skepticism finds footing in attributing dogs' "telepathic" abilities to their sensory skills rather than unexplained forces.

Yet, even as researchers identify sensory explanations for many canine behaviors, some occurrences remain puzzling. For instance, research shows that dogs can often respond to the smallest shifts in scent, emotional state, or movement, but this doesn't fully account for reports where dogs seem aware of a person's arrival without sensory cues. Rupert Sheldrake, a biologist who explored such phenomena, found that a high percentage of pet owners reported cases where their dogs anticipated their return, even at random times and places (Sheldrake, 1999).
While traditional science has questioned Sheldrake's studies, the sheer number of anecdotal accounts has prompted calls for more investigation.

Dogs and Unseen Connections: Morphic Fields and the Collective Unconscious

One of Sheldrake's theories, called "morphic resonance," posits that all living beings, including dogs, connect through invisible fields that allow information transfer beyond known sensory limits. Although this theory is unproven within mainstream science, it aligns with Carl Jung's concept of a "collective unconscious"—a shared reservoir of experiences and knowledge among living beings (Jung, 1969). Jung argued that human and animal behaviors sometimes align because they access archetypal knowledge, connecting them on a subconscious level. These concepts challenge the prevailing assumptions that animals operate solely through learned behaviors, opening a space for curiosity and potential discoveries about unseen connections.

Interestingly, Jung's idea of synchronicity—meaningful coincidences beyond mere chance— also resonates with accounts of dogs displaying "knowing" behaviors. For instance, stories about dogs alerting humans before natural disasters, sensing approaching epileptic seizures, or even seemingly grieving for deceased owners all hint at capacities that elude scientific explanation but suggest interconnectedness. Research continues to explore whether there might be sensory mechanisms we do not yet understand or whether another form of communication exists, albeit one challenging to measure in a lab setting.

Staying Curious Amid Uncertainty

While skepticism guides scientific inquiry, curiosity fuels discovery. History has shown that many once-controversial theories—such as animal magnetism and intuition—eventually found scientific grounding. Today, we understand that dogs can detect human illnesses like cancer through olfactory changes and can sense emotional shifts from hormonal cues. This knowledge was once anecdotal but is now scientifically accepted due to advancements in technology and understanding of animal behavior (Cornell University, 2018). Thus, dismissing dogs' mysterious behaviors prematurely might close doors to revelations science has yet to uncover.

Dr. Alexandra Horowitz, an animal cognition researcher, supports this perspective, encouraging dog owners and scientists alike to maintain an open yet discerning mind. She emphasizes that recognizing dogs' perceptive capacities does not require accepting unproven theories outright but rather invites us to question and study with respect for what we don't yet fully grasp (Horowitz, 2009). This balanced approach encourages a deeper exploration of dogs' abilities, acknowledging that some mysteries remain until science advances further.

Embracing the Mystery

While canine telepathy may remain a subject of debate, there's a beauty in leaving space for the unknown. By acknowledging what we know and don't know, we foster an environment where both science and experience enrich our understanding. Dogs continue to teach us not only about themselves but about communication, empathy, and mutual understanding beyond verbal language. In nurturing this bond, we celebrate our shared journey with these animals, knowing that curiosity and mystery can coexist with scientific integrity.

Through this open approach, we honor dogs as more than pets; they are partners in a journey that defies easy categorization, opening our minds to what might lie beyond our current grasp. Whether science ultimately validates canine telepathy or not, the potential for deeper, more intuitive connections remains a captivating mystery, one that reminds us of the profound nature of the human-canine bond.

Chapter Eleven: A Holistic Approach to Living with Dogs

As our understanding of dogs' emotional and cognitive abilities grows, so does our appreciation for the ways we can nurture and honor their presence in our lives. A holistic approach to living with dogs encompasses more than just training—it's about fostering a relationship built on respect, intuition, and balance. This chapter explores how integrating traditional training methods with non-verbal cues and a compassionate approach can create a harmonious, fulfilling partnership with our canine companions.

Integrating Intuition with Traditional Training

Dogs are incredibly adaptive learners, and while traditional training methods are invaluable, combining these with intuitive techniques can deepen the connection. Non-verbal cues like energy, presence, and subtle body language can support positive reinforcement, helping dogs feel more attuned and responsive. As dog psychologist Stanley Coren explains, dogs' understanding of human communication goes beyond mere commands; they interpret our gestures, eye movements, and even intentions through their acute sensitivity to social cues (Coren, 2004).

Incorporating "silent" or subtle training exercises can encourage dogs to "listen" beyond words. For instance, dogs often learn to read their owners' faces and respond to calm, assertive energy. Cesar Millan, a well-known dog behaviorist, emphasizes the importance of personal energy and emotional balance in training. Dogs mirror our emotions, and maintaining a centered, composed demeanor encourages them to feel safe and grounded, leading to a more cooperative and eager approach to training (Millan, 2007).

Practicing Mindfulness with Dogs

Mindfulness in dog ownership means being fully present in our interactions. Taking a walk without distractions or engaging in a focused play session helps dogs feel valued and recognized. Research suggests that mindful interactions improve dogs' mental well-being, reduce stress, and strengthen the human-canine bond. When we pay full attention to our dogs, they sense it, fostering a sense of security and mutual respect. This "being in the moment" with our pets can mirror the meditative state encouraged in human wellness practices, benefiting us both physically and emotionally (Wells, 2009).

Practicing mindfulness with dogs can also be as simple as observing their behaviors closely without judgment. If a dog seems hesitant or anxious, tuning in to subtle shifts in their body language can provide insight into their state of mind. This observational skill allows us to respond supportively, adapting our behavior to offer comfort or reassurance as needed. The practice of mindful dog ownership can help owners identify early signs of stress or discomfort in their pets, ensuring a proactive approach to their well-being.

The Balance of Training and Connection

Achieving a balanced approach to dog training involves blending structure with empathy. As we employ positive reinforcement, consistency, and patient guidance, it's equally essential to give our dogs room to express their unique personalities. Dogs, like people, thrive when they feel acknowledged and free to explore. Allowing them space to make choices, within safe boundaries, can foster confidence and independence. Balance in training means setting guidelines while respecting their intrinsic nature and recognizing that every dog is an individual.

In her book *Inside of a Dog*, cognitive scientist Alexandra Horowitz explores how understanding dogs' "umwelt"—their unique sensory world—can shift how we interact with them. When we recognize the world from their perspective, we build a bridge of empathy, making communication more effective and meaningful (Horowitz, 2009). By appreciating their sensory- rich environment, we can adapt our training to suit their instincts, creating a blend of guidance and freedom that supports their happiness and development.

Fostering a Lifelong Bond

A holistic approach to living with dogs isn't just about training—it's about fostering a partnership that evolves over time. Building a lifelong bond with a dog means being responsive to their changing needs, adapting our care as they age, and honoring their individuality at each stage. The "golden years" of a dog's life, for instance, might require a shift in activities, such as replacing strenuous play with gentle walks and focusing on comfort and companionship.
Supporting our dogs throughout their life stages creates a bond based on mutual respect, resilience, and trust.

Nurturing the Extraordinary Role of Dogs in Our Lives

Dogs teach us invaluable lessons about empathy, patience, and compassion. They ground us in the present, helping us appreciate life's simple pleasures—a walk in the park, a shared moment of quiet, or a joyful reunion after a long day. This holistic approach invites us to see our dogs not just as companions but as partners who remind us of our capacity for kindness, love, and understanding.

By integrating training with intuition, practicing mindfulness, and fostering a balanced and respectful approach, we create a fulfilling, holistic life with our dogs. This connection transcends words and commands, residing instead in the gentle, knowing moments we share. In nurturing our bond with dogs, we honor them as extraordinary beings who add immeasurable value to our lives.

Chapter Twelve: Closing Thoughts – Embracing The Mystery of Connection

In exploring telepathic bonds with our dogs, the true reward lies not in definitive proof but in the perspective and possibilities this journey brings. This book invites you to approach these connections as an art—one rooted in respect, patience, and curiosity rather than solely in science. When we attune ourselves to our dogs in this way, we enter a unique "bubble" of shared experience, allowing us to see the world from their vantage point and to sense unspoken bonds that transcend traditional communication.

Carl Jung's theory of archetypes suggests that humans may inherit symbolic patterns deeply encoded in our consciousness—universal motifs that speak to shared human experiences (Jung, 1953). It's possible that animals, too, access these archetypes, creating a foundation for empathy and instinctive responses that resonate across species. When we share such non-verbal connections with our dogs, it may feel as though we are tapping into a mutual understanding that bridges the human-animal divide.

An Open-Minded Approach to Connection

The beauty of our relationships with dogs is that they encourage us to explore without needing to understand everything fully. Whether or not we ever confirm the existence of telepathic connections, our experience deepens as we observe, listen, and appreciate the world through their instincts and reactions. Much like other intuitive practices, these moments with our dogs allow us to develop our own mindfulness, enhancing our capacity to perceive the world beyond words.

By trusting this process, we cultivate a deeper, subtler awareness that extends into other areas of our lives. Learning to "send" thoughts or intentions to our dogs may reveal our own hidden instincts, while attuning ourselves to their signals enhances our empathy and connection to the present. In the end, this openness allows us to explore a quieter, more intuitive part of our bond with our dogs, grounded in genuine affection and trust.

Leaving Room for Wonder and Discovery

Engaging in this journey with an open heart lets us appreciate the "how" less than the "what." Dogs, like quiet guides, remind us of the wisdom of intuition and insight—a reminder of Antoine de Saint-Exupéry's words, "It is only with the heart that one can see rightly; what is essential is invisible to the eye" (Saint-Exupéry, 1943). In sharing this space with our dogs, we glimpse a world of unseen communication, where we allow ourselves to be both humbled and inspired by what we don't fully understand.

Ultimately, this journey is less about arriving at a concrete answer and more about nurturing the bond itself. May this exploration with our canine companions deepen your appreciation for connection, not only with dogs but with the world around you. For in cherishing this mystery, we learn to live more fully, guided by love and open to all that cannot be seen but only felt.

Sources:

1. **Beck, Alan M., and Aaron H. Katcher.**
Between Pets and People: The Importance of Animal Companionship. Purdue University Press, 1996.
Insight into the human-animal bond and its psychological and emotional impact, emphasizing the depth of relationships.

2. **Bekoff, Marc.**
The Emotional Lives of Animals: A Leading Scientist Explores Animal Joy, Sorrow, and Empathy – and Why They Matter. New World Library, 2007.
Discusses animal emotions and social dynamics, highlighting dogs' empathetic nature.

3. **Coren, Stanley.**
The Intelligence of Dogs. Free Press, 1994.
A foundational source on canine cognitive abilities and intuitive responses, highlighting evolutionary influences.

4. **Horowitz, Alexandra.**
Inside of a Dog: What Dogs See, Smell, and Know. Scribner, 2009.
A study of the canine sensory experience and perceptive abilities, including dogs' intuitive responses.

5. **Jung, Carl G.**
Collected Works of C.G. Jung, Vol. 9 (Part 1): Archetypes and the Collective Unconscious. Princeton University Press, 1953.
Jung's theories on archetypes and shared consciousness, providing a psychological basis for human-animal connections.

6. **McConnell, Patricia B.**
For the Love of a Dog: Understanding Emotion in You and Your Best Friend. Ballantine Books, 2007.
Insights into human-dog emotional bonds and mutual non-verbal communication techniques.

7. **Miklósi, Ádám.**
Dog Behavior, Evolution, and Cognition. Oxford University Press, 2007.
Examines canine communication, evolutionary development, and social behaviors that foster human-dog bonds.

8. **Nagakawa, Miho, et al.**
"Oxytocin-Gaze Positive Loop and the Coevolution of Human-Dog Bonds." *Science*, vol. 348, no. 6232, 2015, pp. 333-336.
Study from Azabu University on oxytocin feedback between humans and dogs, revealing the hormonal basis of bonding.

9. **Saint-Exupéry, Antoine de.**
The Little Prince. Reynal & Hitchcock, 1943.
The quote about "seeing rightly with the heart" reflects the book's philosophy of open- minded, heart-centered communication.

10. **Serpell, James.**
In the Company of Animals: A Study of Human-Animal Relationships. Cambridge University Press, 1996.
A study on mutual human-animal influences, highlighting dogs' adaptations to human companionship.

11. **Topál, József, et al.**
"The Dog as a Model for Understanding Human Social Behavior." *Advances in the Study of Behavior*, vol. 39, 2009, pp. 71-116.
Research on dogs as models for studying social cognition, focusing on parallels between canine and human communication.

Appendix with Exercises and More

Visualization Exercises

Visualization is a powerful technique that can help deepen the bond between you and your dog by enhancing your silent communication. By creating a clear mental picture of what you want your dog to do, you project this intention through your energy and body language. Here are a few exercises to start with:

1. Picture the Path
This exercise is ideal for preparing both you and your dog for a focused, peaceful walk.
1. **Set the Intention**: Before you head out, close your eyes for a moment and envision the walk. Imagine yourself and your dog moving calmly, side by side, in perfect rhythm.
2. **Visualize the Environment**: Picture your surroundings and imagine how you want your dog to react (calmly passing other dogs, staying close in busy areas, etc.).
3. **Project Calmness**: As you open your eyes, take a deep breath, and keep that vision in mind as you start the walk. You'll notice how your energy affects your dog's behavior.
4.

2. Sending Calm Energy
When your dog is overstimulated or anxious, visualizing a calming environment can help steady their emotions.
1. **Choose a Quiet Place**: Sit with your dog and close your eyes. Picture a peaceful scene—a quiet beach, a calm meadow—anything that relaxes you.
2. **Focus on Breath**: Breathe slowly and deeply. Visualize yourself radiating a calming energy that envelops both you and your dog.
3. **Imagine Calm Behavior**: Visualize your dog lying down quietly, breathing deeply. Hold this vision for a few minutes.

With regular practice, these visualization exercises can enhance your dog's responsiveness to your non-verbal cues, creating a stronger, more intuitive bond.

Exercise in Non-Verbal Commands

Using non-verbal commands strengthens your dog's focus on you, and it often fosters deeper communication. By practicing non-verbal cues, you and your dog can develop a more intuitive understanding. Here's how to get started:

1. Body Language Basics
Start with simple cues for actions your dog already knows, like "sit" or "stay," using only body language.
1. **Sit Command**: Stand still, raise your hand slowly, and hold it with your palm facing up. Use a gentle upward motion to encourage your dog to sit.
2. **Stay Command**: After your dog sits, extend your hand in front of them, palm facing forward, signaling them to stay. Slowly step back while maintaining eye contact.

2. Hand Signals for Common Actions
Once your dog is comfortable with basic gestures, expand to other commands, like "down" or "come."
- **Down Command**: Hold your hand flat and slowly move it downward. This encourages your dog to follow the motion and lie down.
- **Come Command**: Extend your arm out to the side and sweep it toward your chest, inviting your dog to come to you.

3. Practice in Various Settings
Once you and your dog are in sync with these signals at home, try them in different environments. Practicing in new places strengthens your dog's responsiveness and trust in your non-verbal cues, even when distractions are present.
This exercise builds clear communication without words, allowing you and your dog to connect in an unspoken but powerful way.

Exercise in Visualization Practice

Visualization, or "sending," enhances non-verbal communication and builds a unique bond by helping your dog understand your intentions through mental imagery. Here's how to practice visualization with your dog:

1. Start with a Clear Image
Choose a simple action you'd like your dog to perform, such as coming to you or lying down. Close your eyes and imagine your dog doing this action. Visualize them moving toward you calmly or lying down peacefully, focusing on the details of the setting and their relaxed body language.

2. Project Your Intention
Hold the image in your mind and feel the intention you're "sending" to your dog. Imagine this thought moving from you to them as if you're sharing a message.
- **Calm and Confident State**: Stay centered and calm, as your dog is more likely to respond when they feel your focused presence.

3. Observe and Reinforce
Open your eyes and see how your dog responds. If they perform the action, reward them with praise or a treat to reinforce the behavior and build confidence in this shared, intuitive connection.

Visualization strengthens trust and brings a mindful approach to training. Practicing it daily helps you and your dog communicate more deeply, beyond spoken cues.

Exercise in Mindfulness on Walks

Walking with your dog is more than just exercise; it's an opportunity to build trust, stay present, and strengthen your connection. This mindfulness practice encourages you to focus fully on the experience of the walk, creating a shared calm between you and your dog.

1. Begin with a Centered Breath
Before starting, take a deep breath and release any distractions. Focus on being fully present with your dog, leaving behind thoughts of work, errands, or other concerns.

2. Observe Together
As you walk, pay attention to the sounds, smells, and sights around you. Notice how your dog explores with their nose or ears and allow yourself to engage in that curiosity. Walk slowly, if needed, to sync your pace with theirs and enjoy the environment from their perspective.

3. Respond Calmly
If your dog gets excited or distracted, respond with calm energy. Avoid tugging on the leash or giving commands. Instead, breathe deeply, projecting a calm presence that invites them to refocus on you.

This mindful approach not only helps you appreciate each walk but also creates a sense of security and alignment for your dog, reinforcing trust and calm in your daily routine together.

Visualization Practice: Imagining a Calm Walk

Visualization is a powerful tool to communicate intentions and focus your dog's attention. This exercise helps you create a clear mental image that supports a calm, cooperative walk with your dog.

1. Prepare with a Quiet Moment
Before going out, take a few minutes to sit with your dog in a relaxed space. Close your eyes and picture the walk you're about to take. Imagine it as calm, with your dog walking comfortably beside you, aware but relaxed.

2. Visualize Every Detail
See yourself walking confidently, holding the leash gently. Imagine your dog's posture: relaxed, head held steady, tail swinging at ease. Picture how you both move through the environment, interacting with sounds and smells calmly.

3. Practice Before Leaving
Hold this image in your mind for a moment before opening your eyes and preparing to head out. With practice, this mental focus can enhance the walk, helping your dog respond to your calm energy, especially in new or distracting environments.

This visualization exercise is about setting a peaceful tone for your time together. Over time, you may find that both you and your dog look forward to these calm, connected walks.

Exercise: Practicing "Sending" Intentions to Your Dog

The "sending" technique helps build intuitive communication by visualizing and mentally projecting your intentions to your dog. This exercise strengthens the bond and teaches your dog to attune to your cues on a subtler level.

1. Choose a Simple Action
Pick a familiar command, such as "sit" or "stay." Picture your dog performing this action calmly and clearly in your mind. Imagine the scene in detail—see your dog's posture, the setting, and the relaxed energy between you.

2. Project the Intention
Mentally "send" this image to your dog by focusing on the action. Take a calm breath and imagine your dog picking up on your intention, aligning their energy with yours. Visualize them understanding what you want, almost like a telepathic nudge.

3. Observe and Reinforce
If your dog responds, acknowledge it with praise or a gentle reward. Repeat this exercise consistently, gradually introducing more complex actions. Over time, you may notice your dog becoming more attuned to your silent cues.

This exercise encourages intuitive awareness, helping both you and your dog become more in sync through non-verbal communication.

Reflection Exercise: Journaling Your Dog's Intuitive Responses

Keeping a journal of your dog's behavior and reactions can deepen your understanding of their unique ways of connecting with you. By recording moments when your dog seemed to anticipate your needs or respond to your unspoken cues, you'll start to see patterns and refine your own awareness.

1. Choose Key Moments
Select situations where your dog responded intuitively, such as sensing your emotions, reacting to changes in your environment, or following subtle non-verbal cues. Note the details of each experience.

2. Describe Your Own Energy and Emotions
Record your own state of mind and energy levels at the time. Were you calm, anxious, excited? Reflecting on your energy can help identify how your mood and presence influence your dog's responses.

3. Identify Patterns
Review your entries over time to see if there are recurring themes. Does your dog tend to react strongly to certain emotions or pick up on specific cues? Identifying patterns will give you insight into the special ways they connect with you on an intuitive level.

This exercise encourages mindfulness in observing your dog and helps to build mutual understanding through intentional reflection.

Practicing "Sending" Intentions Exercise

This exercise is a core practice to help you connect with your dog on an intuitive level by sending mental images and intentions. It allows you to experiment with "sending" simple, calm intentions, building a quiet but powerful communication style.

1. Start with a Simple Action
Choose a basic command your dog knows well, like "sit" or "stay." Focus on this action without using words or gestures. Picture it in your mind with clarity and calm, visualizing your dog performing the action.

2. Project the Image
Imagine this image being sent from your mind to your dog. Hold the thought gently, without straining or over-focusing. Think of it as an invitation rather than a command, a way to communicate your intention.

3. Observe Your Dog's Response
Stay attentive to how your dog reacts. Did they respond, show signs of focus, or even appear relaxed by your calm presence? Make note of their reaction and refine your technique as you go.

With patience and practice, this exercise can strengthen your ability to connect through non-verbal, mental communication, fostering a bond of trust and understanding.

The "Grounding Breath" for Calm Energy Exchange

This exercise is designed to help both you and your dog feel centered, relaxed, and connected. By practicing controlled breathing, you create a calm environment, making it easier for your dog to feel safe and responsive to you.

1. Find a Quiet Space with Your Dog
Sit or stand comfortably with your dog nearby, preferably in a distraction-free area. Make sure you both feel safe and calm.

2. Take Three Deep Breaths
Inhale slowly through your nose, allowing your chest and abdomen to expand. Exhale gently through your mouth, releasing any tension. As you breathe out, imagine calm energy surrounding both you and your dog.

3. Visualize Grounding Energy
With each breath, imagine yourself rooted to the ground, steady and calm. Visualize this calmness flowing around you and toward your dog, creating a peaceful bubble for both of you.

This exercise helps your dog associate you with calm, safe energy and can be a powerful tool before walks, training sessions, or moments of high stress. It promotes a shared sense of presence and calm that strengthens your bond.

Exercise: "Body Language Reflection"

This exercise is designed to help you become more mindful of your dog's body language, enhancing communication between you. Learning to interpret subtle cues builds trust and makes training more effective by promoting a deeper understanding of your dog's needs and responses.

1. Observe Without Interacting
Spend five minutes simply watching your dog in a calm setting, without giving commands or engaging directly. Notice their natural body posture, tail position, ear movements, and breathing pattern.

2. Mirror and Acknowledge Changes
If your dog changes their posture or expression, try subtly mirroring their movements. For example, if your dog relaxes, relax your own posture. If they become alert, acknowledge this shift by sitting up straighter or becoming more focused in your attention.

3. Reflect and Adjust
After a few minutes, reflect on what your dog's body language might be telling you—whether they seem calm, excited, or cautious. Adjust your own energy or positioning accordingly to reinforce a mutual understanding.

By practicing body language reflection, you cultivate a habit of "listening" to your dog's non-verbal cues, which deepens your connection and improves your responsiveness to their needs. This exercise is ideal for building a balanced, respectful relationship that extends beyond training.

Exercise: "Reading the Room with Your Dog"

This exercise is about becoming attuned to your dog's reactions in different environments and using these observations to deepen your understanding of their social instincts. Dogs are masters at reading non-verbal cues, and observing their behavior in various settings can help you understand their comfort levels, preferences, and potential anxieties.

1. Observe in Familiar Settings
Begin in a familiar environment, like your living room, and take note of how your dog responds to changes in your posture, movement, or voice tone. Does your dog mirror your energy, become curious, or react to specific gestures?

2. Observe in New Settings
Take your dog to a park, a pet-friendly café, or a quiet public space. Watch how they respond to new people, noises, and smells. Notice when they show interest, apprehension, or excitement. Their reactions will often give insight into how they perceive the energy of the place and people around them.

3. Subtle Cues and Adjustments
In each setting, make small changes to your body language, like sitting down, standing, or looking in a particular direction, and watch how your dog responds. This can help you understand the signals they're picking up from you and how they adjust their behavior in response.

By taking time to "read the room" alongside your dog, you develop a mutual language of awareness and understanding. This skill will enhance your ability to communicate in new environments and help your dog feel more secure in your presence, wherever you are.

Exercise: "Trusting the Walk"

This exercise focuses on building mutual trust and allowing your dog to lead parts of your walk, which can deepen your connection and create a more enriching experience for both of you.

1. Choose a Safe, Familiar Route
Begin in a location you both know well, such as a neighborhood path or a nearby park, to ensure safety while your dog takes the lead. Give them freedom (within reason) to explore without constant direction.

2. Allow for Pauses and Sniffing
As your dog walks, let them stop to sniff or investigate areas they find interesting. This exploration allows them to engage their natural instincts and feel a sense of autonomy, which strengthens trust and confidence.

3. Follow Their Lead for Part of the Walk
For a portion of your walk, let your dog lead the way. Keep a light grip on the leash, and simply follow as they move forward, turn, or explore different areas. This shared decision-making can foster a deeper understanding and allow you to tune into their interests and instincts.

By creating space for your dog to take initiative, you show them that you trust their instincts, and you may find new insights into their preferences and personality. This practice strengthens your bond and reinforces a sense of partnership, making each walk a joint adventure.

Exercise: "Mirror the Moment"

This exercise enhances your connection with your dog by mirroring their movements, energy, and pace. It fosters attunement and helps build trust through a practice of shared focus and attention.

1. Begin in a Quiet Space
Find a calm environment where you and your dog can focus on each other without distractions. It can be indoors or outdoors, as long as it's a space where both of you feel comfortable.

2. Observe and Reflect Your Dog's Energy
Take a few moments to observe your dog's current energy level. If they're calm and relaxed, match their energy by sitting quietly near them. If they're excited and playful, mirror that energy with gentle enthusiasm. This mirroring helps create a mutual understanding, signaling that you're attuned to their state.

3. Mirror Physical Movements Gently
As they move, subtly mimic some of their actions. For instance, if they shift positions, shift with them. If they sniff a particular area, lean down and investigate nearby. This mirroring can be light and unobtrusive; it's about showing them that you're fully present and aware of their world.

4. Practice Patience and Stillness Together
End with a moment of stillness, sitting quietly with your dog. This final step reinforces a shared calmness, allowing you to enjoy each other's presence without needing to "do" anything.

Mirroring builds a harmonious connection, helping your dog feel seen, understood, and safe. By reflecting their state and movements, you reinforce your bond through mutual presence and empathy.

Reflection Exercise: The "One-Word Bond"

This exercise centers on associating a particular feeling or intention with a single word that both you and your dog can connect to a shared experience, creating a shorthand for moments of bonding and comfort.

1. Choose a "Bond Word"
Select a word that resonates with a positive, calm energy, like "peace," "together," or "trust." This word will act as a touchstone to bring you and your dog into alignment whenever you say it.

2. Create Positive Associations
Begin by saying this word in a quiet, soothing tone during moments of comfort, such as when your dog is relaxed or sitting calmly by your side. Each time you use the word, follow it with a gentle pat, belly rub, or treat, helping your dog associate the word with feelings of safety and connection.

3. Use in Varied Situations
As your dog becomes more familiar with the bond word, start using it in a variety of situations: when you're sitting together after a walk, during a quiet moment at home, or before bedtime. Over time, the word will act as a bridge, encouraging calm and connection whenever it's spoken.

4. Reinforce Periodically
Revisit this practice regularly to reinforce its meaning. This word becomes a unique communication tool, one that carries emotional weight and reassurance for both of you.

This "bond word" serves as a comforting anchor, helping your dog feel secure and allowing you both to connect through a shared, simple language that reflects trust and affection.

Visualization Practice: "Sending Calm"

In this exercise, you'll use visualization to project a sense of calmness, fostering an atmosphere of relaxation for you and your dog during moments of tension.

1. Settle into Calm
Find a quiet space where you and your dog can sit together without interruptions. Take a few deep breaths to center yourself, releasing any stress or distractions. The more calm and grounded you feel, the easier it will be for your dog to pick up on that energy.

2. Visualize Your Calm Energy
Close your eyes and imagine a sense of calm radiating from you. Picture it as a warm light or gentle wave, extending outward to encompass you both. As you breathe, imagine this energy becoming steady, grounded, and soothing.

3. "Send" the Feeling to Your Dog
Now, focus on your dog and picture them absorbing this peaceful energy. Visualize them feeling relaxed, their breathing slowing down as they absorb the calmness you're projecting. Imagine them feeling safe and secure, mirroring the tranquil energy you're creating.

4. Use a Physical Cue
Gently place your hand on your dog's back or shoulder if they're comfortable with touch. This gentle connection reinforces the calm energy you're sharing. Repeat this practice in various situations, such as before stressful events or in noisy environments, to build a reliable association with calmness.

Over time, this exercise helps your dog learn to associate your calming energy with moments of reassurance, strengthening their sense of safety and trust in your presence.

Practicing Sensory Awareness with Your Dog

Enhancing sensory awareness fosters a deeper connection with your dog and your environment. This exercise engages your senses alongside your dog's natural curiosity, encouraging you both to experience the world fully in each moment.

1. Find a Calm Spot Outdoors
Choose a quiet outdoor area, such as a park, and stand or sit comfortably with your dog. Take a few deep breaths, grounding yourself and focusing on the present.

2. Notice with Your Senses
- **Sight**: Observe colors, shapes, and movement around you. Watch how your dog responds to visual stimuli, like a bird flying by or leaves rustling.
- **Sound**: Listen to natural sounds—birds, wind, distant voices. See if you can tune into your dog's auditory cues and notice what catches their attention.
- **Smell**: Close your eyes briefly and take a deep breath. Imagine how your dog experiences this sense and try to notice scents around you, like nearby plants or fresh earth.

3. Synchronize Breathing and Movement
If you're walking, try matching your pace with your dog's. If they stop to sniff, pause with them and take a moment to experience stillness together.
This exercise builds mindful awareness, creating a shared moment of connection through sensory exploration, helping both of you engage fully with the environment.

Situational Awareness Exercise with Your Dog

Situational awareness allows both you and your dog to be fully engaged in your surroundings, helping to build trust and safety in various environments. This practice is particularly valuable for responsive training and deepening your bond, as it develops both of your attentiveness to each other and the external world.

1. Begin in a Neutral Environment
Start in a familiar place, such as your home or yard, where both you and your dog feel comfortable. From there, gradually move to more varied settings, like parks, trails, or urban areas, to enhance adaptability and awareness.

2. Heighten Your Observation Skills
As you walk, observe the space around you and make mental notes of sights, sounds, and any moving elements. Practice being aware of other people, animals, vehicles, and even subtle environmental changes, such as a shift in lighting or an approaching jogger.
- **Notice Your Dog's Cues**: Pay close attention to your dog's body language as they respond to the environment. Do their ears perk up at a specific sound, or do they glance toward certain areas? This mutual awareness reinforces your connection and enables you to predict each other's reactions.

3. React Mindfully Together
When you notice something that might catch your dog's attention (e.g., another dog approaching), practice calm reactions. If your dog becomes alert or tense, gently redirect their focus back to you, reinforcing calm behavior.

4. End with a Debrief Moment
After your situational awareness session, spend a moment reflecting. Notice if there were any particular signals or moments that stood out in how you and your dog engaged with the environment. This reflection can help improve your mutual responsiveness over time.

This exercise fosters safety, mindfulness, and adaptability, encouraging both you and your dog to stay grounded in a variety of scenarios.

Exercise: Visualization for Behavior - "Turn Around and Look"

This visualization exercise is designed to strengthen your telepathic bond with your dog by practicing intentional visualization that invites your dog to respond to a thought rather than a command. This exercise taps into your dog's ability to pick up on your subtle cues and may help you notice the ways they interpret your energy and focus.

Visualization Technique
- **Goal**: Encourage your dog to turn around and make eye contact or acknowledge you without a verbal or physical cue.
- **Instructions**:

1. **Sit or Stand Quietly**: Choose a calm environment where your dog can focus without many distractions. Let them roam freely, facing away from you.
2. **Clear Your Mind**: Take a deep breath, centering yourself and letting go of any tension. The more relaxed and focused you are, the clearer your intention will be.
3. **Visualize**: Picture your dog turning around and looking at you. See it vividly in your mind, imagining their expression, the moment they turn, and the connection in their gaze. Hold this image for a few moments.
4. **Send the Thought**: Focus on sending the mental image to your dog. Imagine the thought traveling across the space between you, creating an energetic invitation for them to turn and look at you.
5. **Observe**: Stay calm and still. Watch your dog's body language and response. Even subtle changes, like a flick of the ears or shift in posture, may show they're picking up on your intention.

- **Reflection**: Did your dog turn around? If not immediately, did they eventually glance back in a way that felt connected to your intention? With practice, this exercise can deepen your awareness of the ways dogs attune to non-verbal cues and may reveal new aspects of your dog's responsiveness to your focus.

Telepathic & ESP Exercises for Bonding with Your Dog

These exercises tap into the realm of mental visualization, ESP, and intuition to strengthen your connection with your dog. Designed to explore concepts like remote viewing and telepathy, these activities can help you develop a deeper, intuitive awareness with your dog by practicing presence.

1. Hidden Object Visualization
- **Goal**: Build a shared mental image with your dog.
- **Instructions**:
1. Place a small object, such as a toy or treat, in a spot out of sight but within the same room.
2. Sit calmly with your dog and close your eyes, visualizing the object clearly in its hidden location. Imagine your dog finding it, feeling the excitement and joy.
3. Open your eyes and allow your dog to explore the space without verbal commands. Observe if they are drawn to the location.
- **Reflection**: After the exercise, note any specific cues from your dog that align with your visualization. This can help sharpen your dog's focus on subtle cues while allowing you both to explore non-verbal communication.

2. Remote Viewing of a Hidden Person
- **Goal**: Encourage intuition by locating a hidden person.
- **Instructions**:
1. Ask a friend or family member to hide in another room or in a nearby area (indoors or outdoors).
2. Visualize their location, focusing on a mental image of your dog "finding" them.
3. Release your dog and encourage them to locate the hidden person. Observe their body language and note if they seem to pick up on your focus.
- **Reflection**: This exercise highlights your dog's natural scent and tracking abilities while also encouraging mental focus on your end. It's an excellent way to combine practical training with intuitive bonding.

ESP Training Exercise: Remote Viewing for Dogs

Inspired by military research in remote viewing, this exercise encourages you to "send" a mental image of a target location for your dog to find. Remote viewing experiments were originally designed to train human participants in perceiving distant or unseen locations. In this exercise, you'll adapt the concept for your dog by practicing focused visualization and inviting them to search a specific area for a reward.

Exercise Setup
- **Goal**: "Send" a mental image of a hidden object's location, inviting your dog to find it.
- **Instructions**:
1. **Select the Hidden Object**: Pick a small, high-value treat or toy and place it somewhere accessible, like a corner of the room, under a cushion, or near a specific piece of furniture. Make sure your dog hasn't seen you hide it.
2. **Clear Your Mind**: Take a moment to calm yourself, center your thoughts, and build a vivid image of the hidden object and its location.
3. **Picture the Search**: Imagine your dog moving toward the object, sniffing and finding it. Picture their path, the environment, and their expression as they reach the location.
4. **Send the Image**: Focus on mentally "sending" the image of the object's location to your dog, almost as if projecting the thought across the room. Concentrate on a feeling of excitement and encouragement for them to find it.
5. **Release**: Once you've "sent" the image, calmly invite your dog to begin searching, using a simple gesture or word like "find it" while staying calm and neutral.

Observing Your Dog's Response
- **Note Their Search Behavior**: Watch for any immediate or unusual focus on the target location. Does your dog move toward the area you visualized without typical cues?
- **Try Different Targets**: If your dog locates the object quickly, try hiding something else in a different spot and repeat the visualization process to keep building their sensitivity to this technique.

Tips for Strengthening Your Dog's ESP Response
- **Positive Reinforcement**: When your dog finds the target, reward them enthusiastically. This will encourage them to keep participating.
- **Practice with Different Distances**: Gradually hide the object in different rooms or even outdoors, experimenting with how far you can "send" the image.
- **Create a Consistent Routine**: The more you practice this exercise, the more responsive your dog may become to subtle intentions or visualizations, sharpening both your connection and their sensory awareness.

Reflection
This exercise combines visualization and subtle energy awareness, giving you and your dog a way to explore more advanced intuition training. Similar to military remote viewing trials, this activity is about building mental focus, but it's also a reminder of the trust and synchronicity that can deepen through shared exercises with your dog.

Police Crime-Solving Inspired Exercises

These exercises are inspired by techniques used in police K-9 training to improve scent-tracking, recall, and problem-solving abilities. They're adapted to give you and your dog a fun, mystery-themed way to strengthen their skills while practicing some investigative tasks.

1. Scent Discrimination & Object Identification
- **Goal**: Teach your dog to identify and retrieve specific items, similar to how police dogs might search for evidence.
- **Instructions**:
1. **Choose Objects**: Pick two or three different items, like a glove, a hat, and a shoe, and place them in separate parts of a room.
2. **Introduce the Scent**: Allow your dog to sniff each item, giving them time to get familiar with the scent.
3. **Name Each Object**: As they sniff, repeat the name of the item to associate it with the object (e.g., "glove," "hat").
4. **Send Your Dog on a Search**: Place the items slightly out of view. Then, ask your dog to "find the glove" or "find the hat." Reward them with a treat or praise when they successfully identify the correct item.
5. **Increase Difficulty**: As they improve, move the items to new rooms or hide them more creatively. This builds their ability to distinguish scents and remember the names of different objects.

2. Mock Evidence Search with Distraction
- **Goal**: Develop your dog's focus and concentration by searching for a target item amid distractions, simulating a crime scene search.
- **Instructions**:
1. **Choose a Target Object**: Pick a scent-rich item like a sock or a piece of fabric, and hide it in a part of your home, such as under a couch cushion or behind a door.
2. **Add Distractions**: Place other items around, such as toys or other small belongings, to create a more challenging search environment.
3. **Begin the Search**: Give a cue, like "find it" or "search," and encourage your dog to locate the target scent.
4. **Encourage Persistence**: If they get distracted by other items, gently guide them back to the task. Reward them when they locate the target item.
5. **Change Environments**: Try this exercise in different rooms or even outside to build resilience in their search ability.

3. Person Scent Tracking
- **Goal**: Simulate a lost-person search using a familiar scent item, similar to police tracking exercises.
- **Instructions**:
1. **Select a Person**: Have a friend or family member hide in another room or a safe outdoor space, taking an item of theirs (like a scarf) that your dog can sniff before starting.
2. **Introduce the Scent**: Let your dog sniff the chosen item thoroughly, getting familiar with the person's scent.
3. **Give the Tracking Cue**: Use a cue like "find [name]" or "track," and allow your dog to follow their scent trail.
4. **Reward Upon Discovery**: When your dog finds the hidden person, offer them praise or treats to reinforce the successful track.
5. **Extend the Distance**: Increase the distance between your dog and the hidden person over time, or add turns and obstacles to make the trail more complex.

4. Scene Memory Recall
- **Goal**: Enhance your dog's memory and problem-solving by training them to remember specific locations or items.
- **Instructions**:
1. **Set Up the Scene**: Place three or four objects in a specific area of a room, like a chair, a book, and a hat.
2. **Explore with Your Dog**: Let your dog sniff and explore the scene, getting familiar with the layout and objects.
3. **Create a "Change"**: Remove one item while they're out of sight, or switch the position of two items.
4. **Prompt Recognition**: Bring them back to the area and encourage them to explore, noticing their response to the missing or changed item. Dogs may naturally investigate the difference.
5. **Praise Their Response**: Reward your dog for focusing on the change, helping reinforce their observational skills.

7. Remote "Stay" Visualization
- **Objective**: Use mental imagery to communicate a stay or calm command without vocalizing.
- **Instructions**: Imagine a scene where your dog is calm and staying in a specific place. Picture them lying down or sitting with ease. Mentally "send" this image as you subtly give a stay gesture. If your dog responds by remaining in place, reward them with gentle praise, reinforcing their sensitivity to calm, non-verbal cues.
-

8. Imagining an Action Sequence
- **Objective**: Visualize a series of actions (such as fetch, return, sit) to see if your dog follows the sequence intuitively.
- **Instructions**: Picture your dog performing a short sequence, like retrieving a toy, bringing it back, and then sitting in front of you. Visualize each action and imagine your dog completing the sequence with enthusiasm. Say "go" or "fetch" as a cue and observe if your dog follows the sequence you mentally set.

9. Finding Hidden Food with Telepathic Cues
- **Objective**: Encourage your dog to locate a hidden treat with minimal cues.
- **Instructions**: Hide a treat somewhere your dog can safely explore. Visualize the treat and mentally guide your dog toward the location, sending mental encouragement for them to sniff and search. Gently point if needed, rewarding them when they find it, linking the experience to your focused visualization.

10. Detecting a Disturbance Visualization
- **Objective**: Enhance your dog's ability to sense subtle changes by visualizing specific responses to unseen events.
- **Instructions**: Imagine a slight disturbance (like someone approaching from behind) and visualize your dog alerting to it. Picture a light "alarm" in your mind and visualize your dog looking toward the imagined disturbance. See if your dog's awareness increases, connecting your visualization with their natural alert instincts.

Each of these exercises promotes intuitive connection and shared focus, deepening your bond and encouraging a subtle form of communication with your dog. As you practice, stay open to small signals and shifts in your dog's behavior, which may indicate a response to your mental cues.

Mentalizing Excercises with your Dog

Here are some *mentalizing* exercises designed to help you and your dog develop a deeper, synchronized bond by allowing your nervous systems to "merge." These exercises focus on fostering mutual calmness, awareness, and intuitive connection. The goal is to cultivate a space where you both sense each other's states, breathing, and emotions, leading to more harmonious communication.

1. Breath Syncing Exercise
- **Objective**: Sync your breathing with your dog's, encouraging a calm, shared state.
- **Instructions**: Sit quietly with your dog in a comfortable spot. Start by observing your own breathing, then shift your attention to your dog's breath. Slowly begin to match their rhythm, either speeding up or slowing down to align with theirs. Continue for several minutes, creating a gentle feedback loop of calm breathing. This exercise can help regulate both your nervous systems and foster relaxation.

2. Heart Connection Meditation
- **Objective**: Connect through imagining a shared energy between your hearts.
- **Instructions**: Sit near your dog and place one hand over your heart. Visualize a warm, gentle energy extending from your heart to your dog's, filling both of you with calm, supportive energy. Imagine that your hearts beat in sync. If your dog rests or relaxes near you, this indicates a deeper sense of calm. This exercise builds an emotional bridge between you, enhancing your bond.

3. Mirroring Emotions Exercise
- **Objective**: Develop a sense of shared emotions and responses.
- **Instructions**: Pay close attention to your dog's current emotional state (calm, alert, playful, etc.) and consciously allow yourself to feel what they might be feeling. If they're calm, slow your movements and relax your body. If they're alert, try to sense what's catching their attention. Let yourself become a mirror to their emotional state, fostering empathetic awareness that strengthens mutual understanding.

4. Eye Contact and Soft Focus Exercise
- **Objective**: Establish a gentle, mutual awareness by sharing soft eye contact.
- **Instructions**: Sit quietly and softly gaze into your dog's eyes without focusing too intently. Allow your gaze to relax, creating a "soft focus" that invites your dog to settle. If they hold your gaze, allow yourself to feel a sense of connected calm. This exercise encourages trust and strengthens your intuitive link, often resulting in your dog responding to your emotional state.

5. Shared Grounding Exercise
- **Objective**: Promote relaxation and grounding by synchronizing your positions and posture.
- **Instructions**: Find a comfortable, seated position near your dog. Visualize "grounding" energy moving from your feet or seated position into the ground, as if you are both rooted in the same energy source. Allow your dog to feel this calm, stabilizing presence. Take note of how your dog's energy responds, as they often mirror calm grounding by relaxing.

6. Emotional Energy Scanning
- **Objective**: Practice sensing each other's subtle emotional shifts.
- **Instructions**: Sit with your dog and mentally scan your own body for any tension or emotions (like stress, calm, or happiness). Imagine that you can sense similar states within your dog. Try sending a calm, relaxing energy toward any areas of tension they might show (for example, if they're pacing or showing signs of restlessness). This practice encourages your dog to release emotional stress, creating a shared calm environment.

7. Visualizing Calm Environments Together
- **Objective**: Bring yourself and your dog into a shared mental space of calm and trust.
- **Instructions**: Close your eyes and visualize a peaceful place (a forest, beach, or open field) where you and your dog feel completely safe. Imagine you're both there, breathing in the calmness of the scene. Picture your dog walking, sitting, or playing freely. Often, this visualization will bring both you and your dog into a relaxed state, as if you've mentally transported there together.

8. "Pulse of the Pack" Sync Exercise
- **Objective**: Align your physical and mental states with your dog's by creating a sense of "pack rhythm."
- **Instructions**: While walking with your dog, focus on matching their gait and pace, imagining a shared "pulse" between you. As you walk in sync, mentally project calmness and confidence, letting your dog feel steady beside you. Dogs often fall into harmony when they sense a unified "pack" rhythm, which reinforces mutual calm and connectedness.

Each exercise emphasizes calming your mind, observing your dog's behavior, and maintaining an open, receptive mental state. Through consistent practice, these techniques help you and your dog connect on a level that fosters a shared understanding, as if your nervous systems are resonating with each other. This deepened sense of connection can make everyday interactions smoother and strengthen the bond that you share.

Tap into the limbic (emotional) brain for a stronger connection Excercises

Here are some exercises specifically tailored for trainers to better tap into the limbic (emotional) brain for a stronger, intuitive connection with their dogs. Since dogs lack a frontal cortex for abstract planning and decision-making, these exercises emphasize real-time emotional attunement and sensory alignment, fostering limbic synchronization and deeper understanding of non-verbal cues.

1. Mirroring Body Language
- **Objective**: Tune into subtle shifts in your dog's behavior by mirroring their posture and energy.
- **Instructions**: Observe your dog's position, posture, and energy level. Try to subtly mirror their body language (for example, leaning in when they do, relaxing posture when they're calm) without being overly obvious. Pay attention to how their mood shifts when you mirror versus when you maintain your usual posture. This exercise encourages synchronization and helps you become more aware of your dog's subtle movements and energy states.

2. "Non-Verbal Dialogue" Walk
- **Objective**: Foster a rhythm-based connection without vocal cues.
- **Instructions**: During a walk, avoid speaking and focus on moving in harmony with your dog's natural pace. Use eye contact, gentle pressure on the leash, or subtle shifts in body direction to guide them, relying on body language alone. This can help strengthen limbic attunement, allowing you to pick up on your dog's emotional state without relying on verbal communication.

3. Sensory Sync: Scent Focus
- **Objective**: Enhance your understanding of the dog's sensory world through olfactory awareness.
- **Instructions**: Sit outdoors with your dog and focus intently on the smells around you. Notice how your dog responds to scents—watch their nose movements, body shifts, or attentiveness. Mentally note what draws their attention and practice "sending" calm or engaging energy based on their reactions. Over time, you'll find it easier to sense what excites or calms them through shared sensory focus.

4. Heart Rate Harmony
- **Objective**: Use biofeedback to sync your heart rate and breathing with your dog's.
- **Instructions**: Begin by placing a hand over your heart and breathing slowly, imagining each breath as a calm pulse shared with your dog. Over time, attempt to bring your heartbeat and breath rate into alignment with their rhythmic movements, like the rise and fall of their chest while breathing. Dogs often pick up on these shifts, which can help create a unified calm state.

5. Emotion Mapping
• **Objective**: Train yourself to interpret your dog's emotional cues through situational observation.
• **Instructions**: Observe your dog in different settings (new parks, busy streets, quiet rooms) and note how their body language and facial expressions shift. Keep a mental or written "map" of their typical cues—like raised ears, relaxed jaw, or tail position—correlating these with emotions (curiosity, excitement, fear). This "map" can become an internal guide to interpreting their emotions more intuitively, as your brain will start recognizing patterns.

6. "Hold Space" Practice
• **Objective**: Practice maintaining calm, supportive presence without reacting.
• **Instructions**: Sit with your dog in a neutral setting where mild distractions are present. Without intervening or giving commands, observe your dog's reactions to the environment, focusing on maintaining an emotionally neutral state. This exercise helps you practice being present without interference, a skill that builds empathy and reinforces a calm, shared limbic resonance.

7. Feel the Field Exercise
• **Objective**: Sense the "emotional field" or energy that both you and your dog bring into a space.
• **Instructions**: Sit with your dog in a familiar environment. Close your eyes and focus on the emotional tone of the room. Is it calm, excited, tense? Pay attention to your dog's posture, breathing, and movements. Notice if and how your own emotional state changes with theirs. This exercise helps you become aware of the subtle energy exchanges and fosters a shared limbic space, which can later aid in reading your dog's mood changes quickly.

8. Intuitive Cue Practice
• **Objective**: Strengthen intuitive commands through "mentalizing" an action.
• **Instructions**: Mentally visualize a specific action, like your dog sitting or lying down, and focus intently on that thought without verbally commanding it. Observe how your dog reacts over time to this subtle direction. This strengthens your attunement and your dog's sensitivity to your non-verbal cues, especially useful in creating synchronicity without direct control.

9. Silent Shadowing
- **Objective**: Follow your dog without interrupting or guiding, to experience their natural instincts and choices.
- **Instructions**: Allow your dog to wander freely (in a safe area or on a long leash), and follow them without attempting to lead. Observe where they go, what draws their attention, and how they respond to sensory input. This exercise helps you become a passive observer of their behavior, improving your ability to interpret their actions and get into their rhythm.

10. Tactile Mirroring
- **Objective**: Synchronize through shared, subtle touch responses.
- **Instructions**: When your dog leans into you or seeks contact, place your hand gently on their fur, mirroring their movements and maintaining a consistent level of touch. Feel the warmth, texture, and subtle shifts in their body. This physical mirroring taps into limbic sensitivity, enhancing non-verbal communication and trust.

11. Predictive Visualization (Future Event Exercise)
- **Goal**: Practice focusing on an upcoming event to "send" anticipation to your dog.
- **Instructions**:
1. Choose a future activity, like an outing or playtime, that your dog enjoys.
2. At a set time each day, close your eyes and visualize the event happening in vivid detail. Imagine your dog's excitement and energy as though it's happening right now.
3. Pay attention to any behavioral cues in your dog leading up to this event, especially if they seem to anticipate the activity without your normal routine signals.
- **Reflection**: This exercise sharpens your visualization skills and may help you become more aware of your dog's sensitivity to routine and mental energy.

12. Picture the Path
- **Goal**: Navigate with your dog through mental imagery.
- **Instructions**: Before a walk, close your eyes and visualize a specific route you plan to take. Imagine particular landmarks, stops, and areas where your dog might respond or want to explore.

Guided Visualization for Telepathic Connection with Your Dog

Objective: Strengthen your intuitive connection and develop a mental focus that helps your dog "tune in" to you even when you're not giving verbal or physical cues.

Exercise Steps:
1. **Preparation**: Sit comfortably with your dog nearby in a relaxed environment. Close your eyes and take deep breaths to calm your mind. Focus on your intention for this exercise: to connect deeply and intuitively with your dog.
2. **Visualize Your Bond**: Picture an invisible, glowing thread linking your heart to your dog's heart. Visualize this thread as a pulse of energy that flows rhythmically, syncing with your breath.
3. **Project an Action**: Choose a simple action, such as having your dog lie down or move closer to you. Mentally visualize them performing the action calmly and happily. Hold this visualization gently, without forcing the thought.
4. **Open Your Senses**: As you send this thought, pay attention to subtle shifts in your dog's posture, breathing, or gaze. Remain patient and maintain a calm energy as you "send" your visualization.
5. **Reinforce the Connection**: If your dog responds, even slightly, acknowledge it with a quiet "good" or a gentle pet. This reinforces their sensitivity to your non-verbal cues and strengthens your bond.

Reflect: Use this visualization practice a few times a week, gradually working up to more complex actions or scenarios. Over time, your connection may deepen as your dog becomes more responsive to the energy of your thoughts.

Bonus

More inspiring ESP and remote-viewing exercises for dogs

Here's a list of creative and inspiring ESP and remote-viewing exercises adapted for engaging your dog's intuitive and sensory skills. Each exercise incorporates visualization, intention, and direction to see if you and your dog can strengthen communication and mutual focus:

1. Going to a Specific Person Exercise
• **Objective**: Encourage your dog to approach a specific person through focused intention and visualization.
• **Instructions**: Picture a specific person your dog knows (a trainer or family member) in your mind and imagine them at a set location (like in another room or outside). Visualize the person calling or welcoming your dog. Give a command like "find [person's name]," and see if your dog responds to the imagined cue.

2. Avoiding Someone Exercise
• **Objective**: Use visualization to influence your dog to avoid a particular person or area.
• **Instructions**: Picture a person or place you want your dog to avoid, creating a mental image of calm, distant energy surrounding that person or space. Use a command like "stay back" or "no" while holding that image. Notice if your dog resists the urge to approach that person or location, reinforcing the connection between visualization and response.

3. Remote Barking or Alert Exercise
• **Objective**: Practice "sending" an alert to your dog to bark or become alert at a specific stimulus.
• **Instructions**: Imagine a sound or movement (like a doorbell or an approaching person) that would normally cause your dog to bark. Visualize the action and emotion you want them to experience (alertness or curiosity). Try giving a light cue, such as "watch" or "bark," while holding the image in mind. See if your dog becomes more attentive or vocal, even without an actual sound.

4. Object Location Visualization
• **Objective**: Guide your dog to find a hidden object through mental imagery.
• **Instructions**: Hide a favorite toy or treat in a specific location. Visualize the location clearly and the object in place, then picture your dog locating it. Use a command like "find it" or "search," focusing on the hidden item's location. Observe how your dog searches and if they gravitate toward the specific area.

5. Sensing a Friend's Arrival
• **Objective**: Tune your dog's anticipation to a specific person arriving at a set time.
• **Instructions**: If someone your dog knows well is scheduled to arrive, visualize their arrival and picture them calling your dog's name. Try to "send" a welcoming feeling as if the person were already in the area. Note your dog's response and whether they react to your visualization, such as moving toward the door or showing excitement.

6. Guided Path Choice Exercise
• **Objective**: Test if your dog responds to imagined direction during a walk or outdoor play.
• **Instructions**: During a walk, pause and visualize a specific path (like a left turn at an upcoming crossroad). Picture you and your dog moving down that path. See if your dog chooses the direction you're visualizing, showing a connection between your intention and their movement.

Printed in Dunstable, United Kingdom